The Many Sombreros

of

Orvil Reid

By

Don L. Madaris

Contents

This book is dedicated to each missionary, student, pastor, layman, friend, acquaintance, and every other personwho worked with, knew, and loved the Reids.

Thank you for sharing your Orvil-stories with me.

It is also especially and lovingly dedicated to my wife of more than 30 years, Kay Weldon Madaris, who also spent many years working with the Reids in Mexico, and who has patiently shared the full experience involvedin the writing and creation of this book.

PROLOGUE

THE MANY SOMBREROS OF ORVIL REID

"They were expecting us, weren't they Kay?"

"Well, sort of. When I called them last week, I told them we would be here sometime this week. I'm not sure if we ever decided which day exactly."

"OK, I'll knock again."

It was a typically hot late-spring day as Don and his wife stood there at the front door of the small house that sat a driveway's distance from the road, in a crowded subdivision in Ft. Worth, Texas. They had driven down from their New Mexico mountain retreat to spend a few days visiting and talking with Orvil and Alma Reid, about their more than 40 years of living and working in Mexico. He hoped to make their stories available for future generations to read and enjoy. It didn't take but moments outside the comfort of their air-conditioned car to feel the effect of the Texas heat. Fortunately, a large oak tree cast it's giant shadow over the entire front of the house, including the small porch where they were waiting for someone to respond to their knock at the closed storm door. He hoped those inside had heard the knock over the grind of the living room air-conditioner, hanging in a window just off the porch.

Don waited, then knocked again, as he called

out, "Alma, Alma." A time-weary hand pushed aside the edge of the drapes. Half a friendly face slowly appeared in the opening near the edge of the picture window. The eyeball they could see was quickly looking from one of them to the other, seeking some familiar identity before opening the door. The face disappeared, the hand released the drape, and immediately, the door was opened. Alma, still dressed in a floral-print knee-length duster, appeared in the door, shouting their names.

"Katie, Don, I can't believe you caught me looking like this." Her ankle-length nightgown hung way down lower than her duster, but at that moment she didn't really care. She was so excited about their arrival, that even before opening the storm door, she called back into the darkness of the house. "Orvil. Orvil, get up, it's Don and Katie."

They were welcomed like long-lost family members. Non-stop greetings flowed between them, interspersed with questions and answers about life in general. She apologized for her appearance, but they told her she looked wonderful to them. And they meant it. She pulled them into the house, as she continued to talk. The living room was crowded with mementos and pictures from many of the special places their travel and work had taken them. Pictures of children and grandchildren filled the top of the console television and overflowed onto a nearby bookcase. The walls down the hall were hung with framed certificates and gold-edged awards and other important documents, haphazardly displayed for all to see, but lovingly hung there because of the joy they brought to Alma and Orvil every time they walked down that hall. As they saw all those things, they were constantly and instantly reminded of all those other pleasant times in their lives.

Once they were inside the living room, Alma hugged them both again, one in each outstretched arm, as she said, "Why you both look just as young and healthy as you ever did! But Don, when did you grow that shaggy gray beard?"

"Alma, I've tried shaving it off, but it just grows back, so I finally decided the Lord was trying to tell me something, so I let it grow." Everyone laughed, as she insisted that they find themselves places to sit.

"Just move those newspapers down to the other end of the sofa, Katie, and make yourselves comfortable. I need to go help Orvil get presentable enough for company."

"Since when did we get to be company at your house, Alma?" Kay protested. "We don't want to be any trouble for you. Don just wants to spend some time talking to Orvil about some more of the things that have happened in his life, and some of the things he has done which have helped him get to where he is today."

"Oh, he's been looking forward to this time, Don, since the minute Katie called last week saying you were coming our way," Alma added. "He's been dragging out books and pictures and poems. He's been talking a blue streak about things he hoped he'd remember to tell you. Sometimes, he doesn't remember too well these days."

"Sometimes we all have days like that. I hope all this hasn't been too much trouble for either of you," Don insisted, knowing what the probable response would be.

"Oh no, it has been wonderful for him to have something to do. You know someone else tried to write his story a few years ago, but it didn't turn out like either of them wanted it to, so no one ever had a chance to read it."

"I'm sorry. I wasn't aware than anyone else had ever written about Orvil, except Orvil himself."

"Well, he's certainly done a lot of that. I pulled out some folders of his writings and put them there on the table. Look them over while I check on that man."

"Don't wake him up, Alma."

"Wake him up? Why, he's been awake for hours. He just decided to go back to bed after breakfast. But he's not sleeping, he's just being lazy."

They didn't have an opportunity to look at the

folders right then, for as Alma started toward the bedroom at the back of the house, Orvil met her in the hallway, wearing a well-worn running suit and tennis shoes, their untied laces flopping as he walked. All six-feet, 3-inches of him were still there, just a little more stooped and slightly more frail than the last time they had seen him. The wisps of hair above his ears still stuck out on both sides of his otherwise totally bald head, and his bushy eyebrows framed his twinkling eyes, crinkled with grin wrinkles. He wore a big smile, and his grip was strong as he grabbed his friend's arm.

He hugged them and shook their hands several times, while he repeated their names in such a way that made them feel extremely honored and greatly appreciated. He took his place in the room, falling heavily into his favorite easy chair. Alma sat in her own armchair nearby, while Don and Kay found their places back on the upholstered sofa. Orvil knew why they had come, and wanted to get right to the point.

"Now, Don, I understand you want to try to write something about me."

"That's right, Orvil, some of the things Kay and I already know about you make us think others would be interested in reading your story."

"So what do you know about me?"

"For one thing, during your years in Mexico,

you did a lot of things. You wore many hats."

"Except down there, they're called sombreros, Don."

"I remember. So you wore many sombreros. As a student worker, a printer, a writer of poems and plays and books, a preacher, teacher, and many other things."

Orvil eased himself up from his chair, and picked up a large sledgehammer that occupied its own non-assuming place just inside the front door. "Feel that, Don," he said, passing it to his friend. Don took it, pretending it was heavier than it actually was, and looked it over. Orvil said, "Swing it a time or two. But easy. It can get away from you." Don took a couple of light swings, as Orvil continued. "That was the very hammer I used to crack rocks on my stomach. That's probably when I should have been wearing that sombrero shaped like a hard-hat."

"Oh, I've heard about that. It was all part of your strong-man feats. Do you know that's the first think people mention when they hear I'm trying to write something about you? And they also remember something about your letting someone drive a car over your stomach. What was that all about?"

"We'll get to that I'm sure." Orvil put the sledge-hammer back in its special place by the door before taking his place in his easy chair again. "One thing you need to know is that I have my own opinions about anything having to do with trying to write about me. I also have some advice for anyone who might try to write my story. Most people who write biographies give too much credit to the person. If you are going to tell my story, please do it in such a way that it is not so much what I did, but tell how it was such a miracle that the Lord could take a 'nobody' like me, from the 'nowhere' from which I came, and do something with me for His Kingdom."

"I assure you Orvil, I'll do my best to do just that. Alma tells me you've been thinking about some of the things you want to talk about. I don't want to rush you, but are you ready to start?" He nodded yes. As he leaned forward in his chair, the wide-eyed look of anticipation on his face led everyone in the room to believe he was anxious to begin getting some of those thoughts onto paper that had been stacking up inside his head. "Then let me find my yellow legal-pad and a pencil, and my small hand-held tape-recorder, for I know I'll never be able to take it all down, and I don't want to miss a thing." Kay and Alma continued their incidental conversation, as Orvil waited patiently while Don fished his pad, paper, and recorder from the small tote bag he had brought with him. When he was ready, he said to Orvil, "OK, the whole world is ready to learn about the man of many hats, or I should say, about the many sombreros of Orvil Reed."

CHAPTER 1

THE EARLY YEARS

"I've been trying to remember things from way back. It's been a while since I even thought about some of them. But it has been so good to bring them to mind again," Orvil said with a grin. Alma gave Don a knowing wink, smiling in Orvil's direction, as he continued. "The first home I ever knew wasn't much more than an unfinished, one-room lean-to hut in Stigler, Oklahoma, a small community near the Arkansas line. That simple house had dirt floors, which were surrounded by three, rough, un-finished board walls covered with a shingle roof. At the time I was born on May 22, 1908, Christopher Columbus had beaten me to America by only 406 years. Many great Americans were born in log cabins and I always regretted I didn't have the luxury of being born into such a high bracket, but as I understand it, we moved up to that pioneer level while I was just learning to walk."

"Don't forget to tell them about your Indian background Orvil."

"I won't Alma. My paternal great-grandfather was a Cherokee Indian who had been reared with white men. Great-grandfather didn't like the family sir-name of 'Deerman,' so when the time came for him to have it legally registered in order to receive a government land allotment, he officially changed the spelling of the name to 'Dearman'. When I was a boy, that was OK with me, but as I became a jogger and a long-distance runner, I thought the original name taken from that fleet-footed animal, was much better suited to me than the other one."

"And what about your grandfather? And your father?" Alma said again.

"My maternal grandfather had come from Missouri, and family history had it that he was probably of the Jesse and Frank James family, although there are no official family records available to prove that."

"My father, Thomas Wilson Reid, was an almost full-blooded Irishman. His father had only completed a grade school education, but even at that, he was perhaps the most educated man in his community. My father was a hard worker, doing much of his sharecrop work with only one team of mules, a turning plow, a double shovel, and a small harrow. We usually raised hogs for killing at the first winter freeze, in order that we'd have enough lean, cured meat for the beginning months of the harsh Oklahoma winter that almost always came suddenly and stayed for a while. Other than that, we had no meat on the table, except a little sowbelly that was pure fat. We did eat an occasional rabbit, squirrel, or opossum we might kill while working in the fields."

When Orvil was eight years old, his father bought him a .22 rifle. He loved going hunting with his good squirrel dog Old Jack.

"Hey, Dad, with this gun, you'll see that I can be as good as anyone at shooting squirrels. I'll bring them home, skin them, and we'll have them for lunch. I only have one problem -- I'm almost too little to carry my gun and more than two or three squirrels in my hands at the same time."

"Don't worry son, we'll think of something. I remember reading how Daniel Boone and other frontiersmen wore hunting belts, son."

"I like that idea Dad, but there's just one problem. On my overalls, I don't have any kind of belt at all."

"Well, we'll just have to make one. Go get me one of the sacks we use for picking cotton. Maybe we can make you a belt from the canvas shoulder strap off that sack."

"Yeah, and we can tie some short pieces of bailing wire around my canvas belt. Then Daniel Boone won't be the only one coming home with several squirrels hanging from his belt."

"That'll be good son, for our family won't have to wait for hog-killing time to have fresh meat."

"Speaking of eating," Alma interrupted, long enough to ask, "won't you have some coffee and cake? One of our church friends brought us the best carrot cake yesterday. And without some help, we'll just enjoy eating the entire thing ourselves. It's delicious." She didn't even wait for an answer before she was up and into the kitchen, which was separated from the living room only by the open dining room.

"Here Alma, let me help you," Kay said, as she joined Alma in the kitchen. The rattling of coffee pot and plates and forks could be heard over their kitchen-talk, and only accented that which Orvil continued to share with Don. It seems another thing his family didn't lack for was meal.

"Get the mule ready son."

"Where are we going this time, Dad?" Orvil would ask.

"Down to the grist-mill. Mama's about out of meal."

"I love going there, dad. Can I play out by the water-wheel?"

"If you're careful."

The gristmill was driven by an enormous old water wheel. Not only did young Orvil like taking the sacks of shelled corn there on the back of the mule, and coming back with their own fresh ground meal, he liked going to the creek. He liked the squeaking-squawking sound the wheel made with every turn. He liked the whooshing sound as it picked up, then emptied the water each time it made its round.

From the kitchen, Alma called out again, "Don't forget to tell him about your mother, Orvil."

"Oh yes, my mother," Orvil continued. "My mother, Annie Dearman Reid, was her own league of nations. She was a mixture of English, French, Dutch, and was also one-eighth Cherokee Indian. She had a serious health problem most of her life, and being a semi-invalid made our home and family-life even harder. Despite her physical problems, she was an industrious wife and mother who managed to can many of our homegrown vegetables in glass jars in order for us to have enough food to get us through the winter. She also made her own soap for washing the clothes and for taking Saturday night baths."

"I was her sixth child, and the only one to have survived that many years. The first five had either been stillborn, or had died during their pre-school years. From the time I was about eight years old, I was helping my mother around the house. I also helped prepare the family meals on our old wood-burning stove. She had many bad-spell-days when she simply couldn't get out of bed, so on those days she would just say to me, 'Now Orvil, here's what you have to do. Take the flour down from the shelf, then...' Then she'd tell me exactly what to do from her bed, and I would just follow her instructions. As bad as I hated to, I would have to leave her there, because for the rest of the morning I had to help my father in the fields. But I'd always be back at the house before noon to help her finish our lunch."

As Kay came from the kitchen, carrying a tray of cups and plates, she asked, "Wasn't all this awfully hard work for a little boy like you?"

"Yes, but I had to do it in order for the family to keep up with her increasing medical and doctor bills, so I was willing to do whatever I needed to."

Alma followed Kay from the kitchen with another tray, this one with napkins, forks, and spoons and a large carrot cake, divided into generous slices. She served everyone cake, then poured coffee and passed the cream and sugar, as she continued telling Orvil's story. "His father and mother both claimed to be atheists. His father was a militant follower of Robert Ingersol, the great English agnostic unbeliever, and of Voltaire, his great agnostic counterpart in France. I've heard Orvil say how his Father constantly filled his mind with atheistic thoughts.

"A person is just like a chunk of wood, Orvil."

"Do you really believe that, Dad?"

"Why sure I do. Otherwise I wouldn't be saying it. When that chunk of wood is burned up, that is the end of it."

"But Dad, where does God and Heaven fit into all of this?"

"Orvil, there is no such thing as God. Weak and cowardly people have to invent a god to be able to face life's problems. Don't you be one of those weak and cowardly folks."

Orvil would pleadingly look toward his mother, who would always put the conversation off until they were alone together in the kitchen.

"Mother, surely you don't feel this way too?"

"Whether I do or not, son, I have to agree with your father, if for no other reason than to keep peace in the family. You know, Orvil, I had a fine Christian mother who belonged to a Baptist church. And my father never really said there was no God, he just lived as if there was not one."

Orvil's grandfather was also a confirmed gambler, whose luck ran from good streaks to bad.

As they talked, Alma noticed Orvil had hardly touched his cake. "Orvil, aren't you going to eat some cake with everyone else?"

7

"I enjoyed the coffee Alma, but I'd rather talk than eat right now. But you all have another piece. While they ate, he continued with his story. "My bad-living, confirmed-gambler grandfather was also a single-stock double-shovel farmer, with a two-mule team. He owned his own 40-acre farm, which he worked, with the help of my five uncles. He also supplemented his income by making and selling bootleg whiskey. He smoked his own self-rolled cigarettes, made from his homegrown tobacco, but insisted on giving his sons and grandsons a good whipping if he caught us smoking. In spite of everything, he was a good and honest man among his peers, and his word seemed to always be his bond.

"Because we were renters and share-croppers, we moved every two or three years, always looking for a better place to live and farm. Daddy was also looking for a place where Mother might feel better. We lived in places with names like Dry Creek and Greenleaf Creek, and there was also Greasy Creek and the Horn Community – names, which probably revealed more about where we lived than anything else. When I was still a little boy, we moved to a place called Hunger Mountain, where my mother's parents lived. Hunger Mountain lived up to its name too, but at least we were nearer my four uncles and two aunts, who helped take care of Mother.

"I don't guess I was too much different from anybody else who grew up in this kind of home and community environment. I was an under-privileged sharecropper farmer-boy, but I didn't give that idea much thought until a few years later when my Mother's physical condition became so bad that I had to drop out of school when I was just thirteen. I had to go to work fulltime because the food bills and Mama's medical bills were both mounting up. Daddy and I worked ten to twelve hard hours a day during the growing season on the farm, doing everything ourselves -- preparing the soil, planting the seed, then cultivating the crops."

In the summertime, they'd go into the forest and make crosscut ties for the railroad.

"Now this is going to be hard work, son. First we'll have to cut down some trees with our crosscut saw. Then you stand on the log and cut some niches down the side of it with your chopping ax. Then just remove the wood down to the level where you made those cuts on one side of the log. When you do that on all four sides of the log, if you've done it right, you'll end up with an almost smooth, almost square cross-tie ready to be sold to the railroad."

"How much will we get paid for these cross-ties, dad?"

"Oh, about fifty cents for each one."

"If I work about ten hours a day, finishing about eight a day, I can earn five dollars a day. That's a good day's work for anybody."

"And that's not bad, son. Remember the average farm hand doesn't get but about a dollar a day."

"Plus bed and meals, Dad."

"Well, we won't have to worry about a bed, because we'll often stay in the woods, spending nights at the time in a deserted cabin out there. It has very little furniture, but those hard and husky corn-shuck stuffed mattresses on wood-slab beds will feel mighty good after a hard day's work."

"I'm sure anyplace will be better than nothing."

"And when we have enough cross-ties for a wagon load, we'll just take the wagon bed off, and place the ties on the running gears of the wagon, and with the wagon-load pulled by two horses or mules, we'll deliver them to the railroad company and receive our pay."

"Pretty soon, dad, I'll be loading those ties by myself."

"We'll see, Orvil. Just one of them will weigh a lot more than you will."

Orvil's life was busy now, taking care of his mother, working in the fields and chopping trees to make railroad cross-ties, but he never stopped dreaming about the possibility of someday being able to go back to school.

"I didn't have any books at home, and there were no libraries, but I had read how when young Abraham Lincoln couldn't go to school, was able to educate himself by borrowing books from everyone and everywhere he could. So I borrowed a book from somebody titled 'The Giants of The Republic.' It was a book of brief biographies of George Washington, Thomas Jefferson, Abraham Lincoln, Booker T. Washington and George Washington Carver. I was so thrilled by the book and deeply inspired by its stories that I thought to myself, 'If they did it, why can't I?' "

CHAPTER 2

THE HIGH-SCHOOL DAYS

For the first time, Orvil's voice was cracking with emotion, and his eyes brimming with tears. Being the good wife Alma was, she said, "Take a minute Orvil. Let me pour you some coffee. Sip on that while I tell them about that visit your teacher had with your folks."

"Mr. Reid," Alma said, imitating the visitor, "I'm the teacher of the one- room rural school your son previously attended. We've come to your house today with a specific proposal. My wife and I are so sad to see him drop out of school, that we are willing to legally adopt him as our son, in order to guarantee him a good education, including a college education."

Alma changed to the voice of Orvil's father. "I thank you for coming, but neither Orvil's Mother nor I are willing to break up our family. We can't even consider your kind proposal. Son, I can't help you any, but if you work your way, I'll try to take care of family expenses from here out. Your Mother is some better, and maybe we can make it from now on."

They did make it better, but because of their lack of spiritual beliefs, they still didn't go to church anywhere, and probably wouldn't have even if there had even been any kind of church in their community. But one day a traveling preacher came to hold a few nights of evangelistic services in the community's one-room schoolhouse.

"Hey, Orvil, get your shoes on. You and your mother and I are going to that meeting tonight down at the school."

"But why Dad?"

"Well, for one thing, it's just something to do. But then too, we just might find something else we can make fun of."

"They attended the meeting, but something else happened that was totally unexpected. God's Spirit touched his Mother's heart, and she left that service convicted of her sinful condition. The next day, he and his father came in from the fields and found his Mother wandering around the house as though she were in a daze."

"Annie, Annie, what's the matter, Annie?"

"I know this will be a surprising answer to you, Wilson, for you are a man who has said all his life that you are a confirmed atheist, and didn't want any of his family to use the name of God. But Wilson, God has saved me and forgiven me my sins."

Orvil picked up the story again. "Ordinarily, my father would only have laughed at anyone saying such a thing, but this time he was unusually serious about what was going on, why she was feeling that way, and why he was feeling the way he did. That night, all three of us attended the services again, and my Mother was ready to publicly accept Christ as her Savior. When the invitation was given, everyone in the building was surprised to see the two people whom the entire county had heard say, 'there is no God' walk down the aisle and profess Him as their Personal Lord and Savior.   In that moment, I got a brand new set of parents. They had the same bodies, but they were new people inside. The only problem was that they had so filled my head with all negative things about God that they now had problems trying to undo some of the things they'd said."

"Orvil, Orvil. Listen to your father and me. We want to tell you all about God and Christ, and the Salvation He offers."

"No, I won't listen to you. You've told me over and over about how those weak-minded people invented God. I don't want to hear what you have to say now. Those thoughts have been taught to me and ingrained into me, so don't talk to me about God now."

"Orvil, don't be so rebellious. Don't talk to your father like that."

"It's alright, Annie. I just want Orvil to know that there are going to be some changes around here.

We're going to begin to read the Bible, and we're going to be having prayer in our home."

"And your father is thinking about beginning a Sunday School in the community, and if no one else will do it, he'll even be the director of it."

Even though Orvil still didn't believe in their God, he was glad to see a change in their lives and in the atmosphere at home.

There was less anger now. There was less shouting at each other, and they seemed happier and more at peace than before. Perhaps that made it better after all, even if he couldn't accept their Christ and His salvation yet.

Orvil told them about another thing that happened during this time on Hunger Mountain, something that had a life-long influence on his life.

"One of my favorite Dearman cousins got drunk at a country dance, and an argument with his best friend turned into a fight. My cousin was stabbed and he died before anyone could help him. He left a young widow with a newborn baby. His friend was convicted of murder and sent to prison for five years, leaving his wife without a husband and three small children without a father. Men in both families drank too much, and then they threatened to go gunning for the others. They didn't go that far, but they never lived quite as peaceable with each other again. I decided I would do whatever I could to keep people from becoming slaves to alcohol, something I considered a true enemy of the human race. It took a while, but years later, this theme became prominent in the Anti-alcohol Campaigns which I organized in Mexico."

"It's going on noon. I have some cold cuts in the fridge. Won't you stay for lunch?" Alma asked us.

"As much as I like cold cuts, why don't you let us treat you to lunch at the local cafeteria," Kay said.

"That sounds wonderful to me, does it to you, Orvil?" He nodded yes, as she headed down the hall, saying, "But as you can see, I need to get to looking a little better than I am if we're going out where folks can see me."

After a pause, Don said, "But I'm curious Orvil, when did you get back into school?"

"Somewhere during that time, I heard about Dwight Indian School, a Presbyterian mission school, where one could work half a day and then attend classes the other half. I sold my calf and two of my three hogs in order to buy some clothes and books, and to have a little spending money. Then I walked the fifteen miles from our house down Salisaw Creek to the school at Marble City, and was accepted as an intern. Marble City wasn't much of a city however. It had only one store and

16

a post office. The first year, I earned room and board by milking the school's five cows twice a day, and working in the large garden, which supplied the school's vegetables. The school itself was about two miles south of the city, and had a large enrolment of about two hundred students, most of them Indians, representing thirteen different tribes. I felt right at home at the school, for most of our neighbors had been Indians. Besides, I was always proud to claim that I was one-sixteenth Cherokee. The next year, I got a job running the light and heating plants of the school, and I got so interested in electricity that I even dreamed of going on to Haskell Indian Institute to study electrical engineering.

"I tried out for the school's basketball team, and made the team my first year. Though Dwight was a grade school, most of the students were 17 and 18 year old under-privileged fellows. Our athletic teams played in the high-school conference, and we were always at the top of the conference in football, basketball, and track. I was also a member of the track, baseball and football teams, and since there's no one here to dispute my saying so, I achieved a fairly good reputation in all three sports.

"I soon learned that all the faculty and most of the other students were Christians. I began to feel the influence of this strong Christian atmosphere, and knew that those people had something I didn't have. I wasn't living at home now, and I realized something important was missing in my life. One day, Mr. H.C. Hanson, the Director of the School, came to talk to me.

"Orvil, you've been studying here with us for several months now. You've learned some important things that will stay with you for the rest of your life, but there's one thing I want to share with you that will change the rest of your life. Will you listen?"

"Sure, Mr. Hanson. But what is it?"

"Some of the other boys told me what you thought about God and Jesus."

"That's just what I was always taught, Mr. Hanson."

"But you don't really believe that anymore, do you, Orvil?

"I guess not."

"Well, what I want you to know is that God is real. And He did send His son Jesus, to live here and to die for us, in order that we might have the kind of salvation that would strengthen us and give us a hope not only for now but forever. It's so simple, Orvil. Would you be willing to let Jesus come into your heart and be your Savior today?"

"I've been wanting someone to ask me something like that. Yes, Mr. Hanson, I want to ask the

Lord to forgive my sins and become my personal Savior. But what do I do now?"

"You've already done it, Orvil. And sometime later, the presbytery of the church will talk to you about becoming a member of the church. If you agree to that, you will be sprinkled into the Presbyterian Church, the only one we have around here right now."

At the end of his second year in Dwight, they announced that the school had changed it's policy and was not going to teach students past the ninth grade, so Orvil knew he would have to find another school for the upcoming year.

"As I had become a pretty good athlete, I wasn't surprised that both county seats near Dwight began to scout me and encourage me to attend their schools. It didn't hurt my chances much, when in the last game of Dwight's football season against our rival, Stilwell, I caught the touchdown pass that won the game for my team. Stilwell was the school about eight miles from where my parents lived, and the Stilwell sports fans wanted me to attend their school."

"Orvil, if you'll come to Stilwell next year, we'll find you a place to stay where you can work for room and board. What do you say about that?"

"I agreed to do so, and enrolled for the following year. When school started, they still hadn't found me a place to live, so I had to have a talk with the coach.

"Coach, I've stayed for after-school football practices so far, but that means a 16 mile round-trip jog to and from home, so as much as I want to stay, I'm sorry I'm not going to be able to continue."

"Let's don't be too hasty, Orvil. I've heard Dr. Church, a hearty supporter of the Stilwell team, is looking for some young man to live with them. He wants someone to clean his office, and help his wife around the house. What do you think about that?"

"As long as they really need someone to do the work, I'll at least be earning my keep."

Orvil later moved in with an insurance agent and his family, who really did need some help. Mr. Dawson was a Deacon in the First Baptist Church. Since coming from that militant atheistic home, Orvil knew nothing about churches, but as he began attending the Baptist Church with his new family, he came to know and accept the Lord in a more personal way.

"I wanted to follow Him in baptism, so one cold winter day, they broke the ice at the edge of the creek, so I could enter the water and be baptized into membership of the First Baptist Church. I was soon involved in Sunday School, B.Y.P.U. -- that's Baptist Young People's Union -- and I even preached at times. I also became the teacher of my own youth class, sang in the choir, and was part of an evangelistic youth team that conducted services in pastorless churches, missions and rural schools. While I was still in high school, First Baptist Church also licensed me to preach.

"These were hard years and I felt Brother Dawson was making too much of a sacrifice by continuing to support me, so I rented a room with three other boys who lived in the rural school district and needed a place to stay in town. We found extra work keeping some offices clean and firing up their boilers in the winter before the other workers arrived. I was nearing graduation from high school, almost before I realized it.

"One of the activities I look back on which gave me invaluable experience later in life, was when I initiated the publishing of a bi-monthly school newspaper. The editor of the County Weekly Newspaper printed it at a very low cost, although I did the writing, the editing, helped with the layout, and even sold advertising to pay the bill. When I began the Student Home Print Shop years later in Mexico, I saw how the Lord had helped prepare me, by teaching me so many things through that school newspaper.

"Stilwell never had a track team, but I got someone to give me four pine boards about three and half feet long, and I made three high hurdles which I set up on an unused dirt road near our house. I practiced with them every afternoon, until I felt I got good enough to compete in several cross-country track meets.

"As graduation from high school approached, I had two real problems. I was president of the graduation class, but I didn't even have a suit to wear for graduation, and was embarrassed to think of wearing my old blue denims and my cotton sweater. Because I was the president of the senior class, the ring company gave me my class ring. I also won a $20 gold piece that the Chamber of Commerce presented to an outstanding student, but I still found myself in something of a dilemma.

"The Oklahoma State high school track meet was be in Stillwater that year, and I wanted to participate. The local bus company only ran to the county line, but when they found out what I wanted to do, they gave me a free ticket there, and some of the sport's fans gave me money to get additional connections on a cross-state bus. On the day of the tract meet, I got to the end of the line, only to find that the cross-state bus would not be coming through for some three hours, so I hitchhiked a ride and got to the University at Stillwater in time for the meet. While there, a newfound friend shared his room with me, and allowed me to join him for meals in the college cafeteria. Because I had very little money, these were special blessings. After the meet, we both hitchhiked back home to Stilwell. It was then that I discovered that I had saved enough money to buy a cheap suit of clothes and graduate in style.

"The years had rapidly passed, and I was all too suddenly ready to graduate from high school, the first person in my family to do so, and as far as I knew, the first in my rural school district to even attend high school. By attending one session of summer school I had finished four years of high school in three years. My two years at Stilwell had been happy ones. Other than all my church activities, I'm proud to say I sang in the high school glee club and the male quartet, took part in the annual class play, and earned 13 letters in football and basketball.

"Because I was on the football, basketball, and track teams, I found the usual bevy of flappers competing to see who would be my girl. I reacted negatively to the efforts of those whom I thought to be frivolous, but Wynona and Jewell were two very quiet and serious girls in my class, who were from the prominent Starr family. As with most people from Oklahoma, they were also one-fourth Cherokee Indian. I finally got the nerve to ask the younger Wynona for a date to church, but she turned me down. Then I asked her sister Jewell, who accepted. Soon we became regulars at church affairs, and she at last invited me home to meet her family, who lived at Starr Springs, about three miles from town. I was sort of already in love with Jewell. That day I fell in love with the whole family, and that love continued to grow.

"After graduation, people kept asking me what I was going to do, now that I had finished high school. Some had asked the same question after I finished grade school. No one understood my desire to continue learning. When I replied that I was going to study at least four more years in college, someone seriously asked me if I was going to attend school all my life? If they'd only known that I would not only attend those four years at Oklahoma Baptist University, but three more years at Southwestern Baptist Theological Seminary following that, then study at the Mexican National University in Mexico one full year and three summers after that, they would really have wondered about me.

"I sold the few hogs on the farm that were considered mine and left for Oklahoma Baptist University, arriving in Shawnee on September 1, 1929, with a hundred twenty dollars in my pocket. Two scriptures came to be of special significance to me. Philippians 4:13 says, 'I can do all things through Christ who strengtheneth me.' Philippians 4:19 says, 'My God will supply all my needs according to His riches in Christ Jesus.' These verses kept me going many times, when it seemed all the possibilities were impossibilities and all the doors were shut."

Alma joined them in the living room again, now dressed in a pretty dress, with her hair and face all prettied up as well. "Anybody hungry?" she announced. "You better be, because I'm about to wrap-up this part of the story of Orvil Wilson Reid before we go eat.

"Before he left for Oklahoma Baptist University, he and Jewell Starr became officially engaged to be married. At about the same time, she left to attend Baylor College for Women at Belton, Texas, which was later changed to Mary Hardin Baylor University, but he tells me they wrote to each other all during their college years. It was at OBU that he really began to see unusual spiritual growth during these early ministry years. Now let's go eat."

As Don helped Orvil up from his easy chair, he asked, "Alma, when did you come into Orvil's life?"

She grabbed her purse from the kitchen table, bent down to tie Orvil's tennis shoes, as she said "Oh Don, that's another long story for another day." Orvil did something he did every time he went out the front door. He reached out and lovingly touched the large sledgehammer standing there by the door, and they were all off for the cafeteria, to continue talking about the many sombreros of Orvil Reid tomorrow.

CHAPTER 3

THE EARLY MINISTRY YEARS

The following day Orvil was up early, and had already had his bath, shaved, and was anxious to get down to business the minute Don and Kay got to their house around 9:30. He greeted them, and then quickly said, "Get out your legal pad and tape recorder. I'm anxious to continue reliving my life with you." It didn't take Don but a few minutes to get set up. And it didn't take Orvil but a minute to pick up his story right where he'd left off the day before.

"As thrilled as I was to be attending Oklahoma Baptist University at Shawnee, it was hard for me to leave Stilwell. I'd made wonderful friends there. Furthermore, it was at Stilwell that I had encountered the Lord in such a genuine and personal way. It was there that I'd gotten active in First Baptist Church, which had done so much to nurture me spiritually, as well as license me to the Gospel Ministry. But I'd already learned that life was never static, and that forward progress was essential in order to get ahead in life. I had to remember that scripture which reminded me to forget some of the things behind me and press on.

"I arrived at OBU with my pockets full of

27

emptiness, but with my heart full of faith, that by God's Grace I'd somehow be able to stay in school. Shortly after arriving, I was blessed to meet a wonderful elderly, Christian widow-lady, who lovingly opened her home to preacher boys of the University, charging them only what it cost her to feed them. I got a job at a used furniture store, at the overwhelming salary of twenty-five cents an hour. I worked a four-hour shift, five days a week, but was glad to get that one-dollar a day paycheck. That first winter in college, a blizzard hit Shawnee. Everyone was snowed in. The owner of the furniture store closed the store for the week, since it was so cold, and with the snow so deep he was sure people would not get out in such weather.

"He paid me five dollars for the week anyway. The school had given me the privilege of paying my tuition every week, so after using part of that money for my tuition, and using some of it to pay my part of the grocery bill, all that was left by the following Sunday was seventy-five cents, fifty cents of which I held onto as my tithe. This was my first big tithing-test. For years after becoming a Christian, no one had ever spoken to me about tithing, although I'd heard it mentioned in a sermon that a faithful Christian should give at least a tithe – or ten percent – back to the Lord. I had heard some pastors complain from time to time, that members were not giving enough to sustain the church budget, but they said nothing of God's plan of tithing and offerings to support his Kingdom work. I learned more about tithing when my youth group presented a stewardship play to the church titled *The Robber, Deacon Brown.* The play presented the critical needs of the kingdom, and dramatically demonstrated the fact that most church members were robbing God his holy tithes, at the same time giving nothing as an offering of love, causing disaster in the work of the kingdom. Not only was Deacon Brown convinced that he had been committing the horrible sin of robbing the Lord who had given his all for him, but robbing the tithes that God says are plainly His. The play also emphasized the truth that it is a spiritual crime to rob God, for it also robs people of the opportunity for eternal life, and deprives the 'robber' of many rich blessings that God wants to give him, but cannot, until he repents of his sin, and stops doing it. As a young Christian, I had become convicted that I too was robbing God, and I determined I would never do it again. That big snow and all its difficulties presented me with a different set of circumstances and a totally different perspective on giving my tithe.

"As the offering plates were passed at church that Sunday, the Devil kept saying to me, 'If you give that fifty cents as a tithe, how will you eat all week on the twenty-five cents left over? Furthermore, what about your tuition for next week?' There was a real temptation to hold on to that money. After all, I was sure God understood something of my need. Wouldn't He let me by just this once? I took the offering plate with one hand, and thrust my other hand into my pocket, fully intending to wrap my fingers around and firmly hold onto that fifty-cent piece, intending to do all within my human power to keep from giving it to the Lord that day, but before I realized it, I had already put it in the offering plate. What I felt was a feeling of relief from the temptation more than a feeling of disappointment. Although I was not actually worried about it, one of my first thoughts was 'How AM I going to eat for the next few days?' Some students received invitations to share fellowship and mealtimes in church members' homes, but for some reason I had never been invited out to eat with any of the church people. To my surprise, as I was leaving the sanctuary after church that very day, a family I barely knew invited me to eat with them at noon. When we sat down at their sumptuously loaded table, they asked me to say the blessing. It was one of the most genuine and most sincere 'thank you for this home and this meal' prayers I had prayed in a long time. The meal was such an ample one that I didn't even have to think about eating that night. Once again, the Lord had proven his faithfulness to me, after I had been faithful in giving Him what was rightfully His.

"The care-taker at the University loaned me a shovel and for the next few afternoons, I spent my spare time shoveling snow from walks and driveways. The temperature was well below zero, and since I had no overshoes or earmuffs, I tied some old sacks around my feet and a woolen rag around my head to cover my ears. Many of the people who lived close to the campus lived in fine homes. I would boldly knock on their doors, or ring their doorbells, and ask if they would allow me to clean the snow from their sidewalks. Perhaps because they felt sorry for me, or perhaps because they genuinely needed the job done, I got all the work I could handle. When I'd finish a house, I'd knock at the door again, announcing that the job was complete. When they asked what they owed me, I learned that saying, 'Just pay me whatever you think it is worth to you', was much better than quoting a price. Many of them paid me much more that way than they might have done otherwise. And too, after awhile, the activity of shoveling snow actually made me feel warmer. At least I forgot about being so cold. Maybe doing some good for other people had something to do with it as well. And of course, the money I was earning helped warm up my pockets too, although with the need to pay the school, eat, and continue to buy school supplies, even that extra money didn't last long.

"It was during those days, when I literally didn't have but a few pennies to my name, that I received a surprise visit from Professor Humphries, my old coach from elementary school days. He arrived at my boarding house with a welcomed gift of fresh fruit. Before he left, he asked me if he could read a passage or two from my Bible. After he left, I enjoyed some of the delicious fruit, but still didn't know what I was going to do for the rest of the week. Before I went to bed, I opened my Bible to re-read that same passage, and I found a five-dollar bill folded in there. Coach Humphries must have left it for me, without even saying a word about doing so. As far as I ever knew, my coach had done so without knowing of my desperate need for money at that particular time in my life. Perhaps, being the sensitive man he was, he simply knew how it always was with college students."

Kay chimed in saying, "And the Orvil Reid I know, has remembered that kind gesture many times, and has tried to repay it over and over again, by passing it along as he helped so many others in so many ways in his life."

Orvil's face turned red all the way to the top of his head. "Alma, please get me a handkerchief." She did so as she continued to talk, while Orvil patted his face and dabbed at his watering eyes.

"Some of the things Orvil began to attend were the Noonday Prayer Meetings conducted by OBU students. In order to gulp down his lunch at Widow Thompson's house, he literally had to run there after his class, following which he had to complete his assigned task of cleaning up the kitchen and tables, and washing the lunch dishes for the other fifteen people, before running back to arrive at the prayer meeting just as it was starting. But those Prayer Meetings met a genuine spiritual need in his life. The fellowship with other Christian people in that setting was exactly what he needed at that particular time in his life. In his second year at O.B.U., he even became the leader of those noon-day prayer meetings."

When Orvil was able to speak again, he said, "I also joined the Mission Volunteer Organization, as I felt a great interest in learning more about World Missions. We not only met as a group, but tried to reach out individually through an extensive local missions program, which often averaged more than a dozen services each week in various places. One week, we received permission to hold services on a creek-bank inside the city limits where a group of homeless people lived, cooking their food in tin cans and sleeping out in the open air. Because of the transient nature of the group, the students decided to continue these services and the contact with the people who came and went there. As winter came, we became concerned, and appealed to the City Council to give us permission to invite these homeless people to sleep in the basement of the City Hall where the boilers that provided heat to the entire building would keep them warm. We couldn't stand the thought of them nearly freezing to death on that bitter cold creek-bank.

"We got permission, and as part of our program we continued to hold evangelistic services with the people in the basement of that building. The service always concluded with an invitation to all of those who would like to know more Jesus and about how to be saved. On one of those cold nights, when the basement was almost full of people, an elderly man came forward and said to me, 'Mister, I am eighty years old, and have been a bum for most of those years. I have been in every city of any size that there is in these United States; I have been in churches of all kinds in all my years, but this is the first time that any one has personally tried to tell me how to be saved.' I explained the Plan of Salvation to him and he received the Lord, and the new hope born in his heart could be seen on his face, as he thanked the Lord for the New Life he had received. I'm convinced that it is never too late or never the wrong time or never the wrong place to witness to people about the Lord.

"I also had the opportunity to formally preach in missions and was finally called to pastor a little rural church. The University Baptist Church of Shawnee ordained me in November of 1930. As director of Missions of the Baptist Student Union at the University, it was a new experience for me to organize 21 simultaneous cottage revivals in the city. We presented a radio program at 7 PM, then went to churches, homes, vacant buildings, and vacant lots for services at 8 PM. All those experiences proved to be of great value later on the mission field. I realized early in my life that one could be a real missionary at home, in high school, or at college, and I knew that anyone who was not a missionary at home would not be a missionary anywhere else. If God was ever going to use me as a missionary in another place, he wanted me to begin to serve where I was right then. So I did!

"While I was still a junior in college, the two small, half-time churches of Pernell and Countyline, Oklahoma called me to work with them as their pastor. After only six months the Countyline church became a fulltime church, and I don't think I've ever seen a more consecrated group of people than the members of that oil-field church. The members were intensely interested in proclaiming Christ in a personal way. The women of the church never went anywhere without a copy of a Gospel tract in their purses, and the men carried one in their shirt pockets or in the glove compartment of their cars. This sense of consecration didn't stop with the adult Christians. We organized noon-day prayer meetings in the Alma high school, the one most of the church's young people attended, affording them an outreach into the lives of their young friends in a way they never knew was possible. Even the grade-school children felt the need to reach out in the name of Christ, feeling that if the University where their pastor studied, and the high school where their older brothers and sisters and friends attended, could conduct noon-day services, they could do the same. They received permission to use one of the classrooms at noon, and one of their Baptist teachers, Miss Beatrice Denny, was chosen as sponsor. Revival was happening in the lives of people all over the Countyline Community, and it was a wonderful thing to sense, experience, and see.

"One man, Ollie Jackson, the personnel manager of a large oil company in the community, was a man of influence, and was respected by everyone, but he had never accepted Christ, even in the midst of the spirit of revival which was sweeping through his community. Being a good friend of the Jackson family, I went to see them often on the weekends when I came in from OBU. Their daughter, Opal, overcame the indifference of her parents, and accepted Christ during a Sunday evening worship service. Following the service, she was overjoyed, and insisted that I come back to her home with her, saying, 'Brother Reid, I want you to pray with my father and mother, so they will be saved too.' When we arrived at her house, her parents were already in bed, but since they considered me more like a family member than a guest, they invited me to come right into their bedroom and talk. When we walked into their room, little Opal flung herself into her father's arms and cried out this message on his shoulder."

"Daddy, I was saved tonight. I would not have been saved if I had listened to you, for the old Devil made you tell me not to go to church tonight, and you didn't agree to it until I cried to go. I want you and mama to come to Jesus too."

"The situation was somewhat awkward, so I asked, 'May I return tomorrow morning to talk and pray with you?' "

"Certainly, Brother Reid."

"I arrived at their house early on that Monday morning, but only Opal and her Mother were there. Mrs. Jackson had been a member of another church, but realized that morning that she had never really accepted

37

Christ as her personal Savior. She admitted that she had been ready to do so before, but was waiting for her husband to make his decision. I found him at the oil camp, and although he was working in his pick-up truck, doing all the supervisory things he had to do, his heart seemed touched by what I shared with him that morning, and he admitted his need to give his wife and daughter a Christian husband and father. He promised that he would give the matter some serious consideration, also promising that the entire family would be in church services the next weekend.

"The following week, I couldn't get Ollie Jackson off my mind. About two o'clock one morning, I felt the need to write Mr. and Mrs. Jackson this letter. 'I can't tell you how happy I am that Opal now has eternal life in Jesus, and will have the Lord to guide her throughout her life. What she also needs and wants however, is to have a Christian father and mother to help her reach her potential in life. Mrs. Jackson, I know you said you were ready to accept the Lord, but that you wanted your husband to go with you. Mr. Jackson, you said you would seriously consider the changes you needed to make in your life. My prayers are with you all of you during these days.'

"True to their promise, the entire family did attend the services and the entire congregation was thrilled when all the Jackson family publicly indicated their desire to receive Christ as their personal Savior and asked to be baptized. Ollie Jackson, the farm boss, had about forty men working with him. In the year following Mr. Jackson's conversion, twenty-seven of those men also accepted Christ and were baptized. A few months later, many of the oil people were moved to a new oil field, where the church had a small mission with a Sunday School. Ollie became the Director of the Sunday School, and the layman in charge of this mission, and served faithfully until his death a few years later.

"After I had already served several years as a missionary to Mexico, I went back for a visit in the Jackson home. Opal was now married and lived in another state. The widow Jackson lived alone. After talking a while about the old times, Mrs. Jackson said to me, 'Bro. Reid, I want to show you one of my dearest treasures.' She brought out a small metal box, what she called her treasure chest, and pulled from it the letter I had written them in the early hours of the morning, many years before. She said, 'If you had not visited us, and later written this letter, my husband would probably have been lost forever instead of now being in Heaven, and Opal and I would not have had the blessings of salvation for all these years. Thank God for what you did for us.'

Just those words would have repaid me well for the four years of my life given in the Lord's work in that wonderful little church at Countyline.

"After graduating from Oklahoma Baptist University, it was still my joy to continue pastoring the Countyline Church for two more years after entering Southwestern Seminary at Fort Worth. At the end of my first year in Seminary, I married Jewell Starr, my high school sweetheart from Stilwell. She had already graduated from Baylor College for Women at Belton and had already finished one year at the Seminary.

"After my second year of study in the seminary and a four-year pastorate at Countryline, I was called to pastor the First Baptist Church of Pryor, Oklahoma. The agreement with the church at Pryor was that I be permitted to continue my studies in the seminary. However, as the responsibilities of the church grew and the constant traveling between the church field and the seminary eventually became too much, we prayerfully decided to devote ourselves full time to the work of the church. It was during that year at Pryor that our only son Roderick was born.

"Even though the decision to leave the Seminary for a time was a joint decision based on the leadership of the Lord, both Jewell and I continued to feel convicted that God was calling us to the Foreign Mission Field.

We knew there were many without Christ here in our own country, but we felt most of them could have heard the Gospel if they had wanted to. In many other countries of the world, there was often not one born-again Christian witness in every thousand citizens, and not one Baptist preacher per million people, so we made formal application to serve as missionaries with the Southern Baptist Foreign Mission Board. I knew I would have to be educationally prepared to go to the mission field. That meant I had to finish my Master of Theology degree in the seminary in order to be appointed. Jewell had already finished a two-year course for her Masters in Religious Education. So in order to return to Seminary as full-time students, we resigned the Pryor Church after a pastorate of only two years. Our long-range plans included moving out of the parsonage at Pryor at the end of that year, but unfortunately, the parsonage burned to the ground on Christmas Eve night and most of our furniture and personal possessions were lost in the fire. The church replaced many of those things before we moved back to Ft. Worth in order to take some of the final steps that would lead us further down the road to Mexico.

"The day before the fire, we took my fifty-four year old father to a medical specialist because he had been complaining of some serious-sounding physical

41

symptoms. When the extensive exam was over, and the lab report came back, the doctor told me, 'Mr. Reid, your father has cancer in the last stages. He doesn't have very long to live, maybe no more than two or three months. There is nothing medically we can do for him. It may be better if you do not tell him, but you will have to make that decision.'

"My father immediately asked about what the doctor told me. 'You know Dad, I promised to tell you the truth, good or bad, knowing you will be able to deal with it better if you know.' So I told him as gently as I could, but added, 'You know Father, doctors can be mistaken.' "

"That's all right son," my Dad lovingly responded. "If this had happened ten years ago, before I knew the Lord, it would have been a different matter altogether, but now it only means I will leave my sufferings and sorrows to be in perfect happiness forever. If all this had happened before I was saved, it would have been tragic. Now it isn't that at all. I could worry about your mother and your little brother, but the same loving Savior who will care for me in death will care for them in life." In the following months, my Dad consoled many people whose intention had been to try to console him. One day he said to me, 'Son, I want you to know that I don't want sad songs to be sung at my funeral. If you have anything to do with it, sing songs of joy, sing songs of triumph and victory. People are going to see my dead body, and some will say that they saw me at my funeral, but they will not see me there. They will only see the house in which I lived on earth. It would be ridiculous for my family and friends to be down here weeping for me, when at that very moment, I will be rejoicing with the Lord in a way I never dreamed of doing on this earth.' "

"Jewell and I knew that at almost any time we might receive a notice from the Foreign Mission Board informing us that we had been accepted as missionaries to Mexico. That would mean we would have to leave Father in that critical condition. We knew we really couldn't be of any further help to him, except to give him support by our presence and our prayers. Dad made it so much easier for us by saying, 'Son, if the Mission Board gets ready for you to go to Mexico, don't wait a single day because of me. The people in Mexico need you now to take them the words of eternal life, and you cannot really do anything else but that which God has called you to do.' "

"The Lord resolved any problem all of this may have caused by calling my father on to his reward before we needed to leave for mission appointment. Dad's faith had grown stronger with each passing day. Just as he had said, only his earthly house was left empty. The funeral service was held in the First Baptist Church at Stilwell, the same church that had baptized me, and licensed me to preach. For the burial, his body was taken to a small rural cemetery nearby where several of his children who had died in infancy, were buried. Many people from all over the state of Oklahoma attended the funeral service at the church. Several of our friends accompanied us to the little country cemetery.

"When we arrived at the cemetery, the other friends who were digging the grave told us they had run into almost solid rock and that the grave was not ready. It looked like it might be an hour or more before we could continue with the gravesite service. My mother's father had come with us, as well as several other unsaved men who had known Dad through the years. My bad-living, easy-gambling, whiskey-making old reprobate of a grandfather had been greatly impressed by the change in the lives of my father and mother, after they had accepted Christ as Savior and Lord at that Revival meeting many years before, but he had continued to live his old sinful and hard life. My Dad dearly loved his father-in-law and had done all within his power to win him to the Lord during his lifetime.

"My father's unsaved friends had also heard the gospel from him many times, but without any success as far as anyone could observe in their lifestyles. While we were waiting, some of the church-going crowd who had come from the funeral service at the church began to sing some of those great old hymns my Dad had loved. I felt an overpowering feeling that God wanted me to preach an evangelistic message while we waited for the gravediggers to complete their job. When the invitation was given at the end of that impromptu service, not only did my grandfather accept Christ, but twelve of my father's other unsaved friends as well. What great rejoicing there must have been in the presence of the Lord, with my own father rejoicing the most, as he thanked the Lord for calling him to Heaven, so his own father-in-law and all those friends might hear the gospel preached one more time while waiting for the men to complete the digging of his grave in order that they could bury his earthly temple. In doing so, they had finally found the way to eternal life through that particular and unusual set of circumstances.

"What a great difference there is between life and death. What a contrast in the value of the Christian faith over the cold, dark, hopeless, materialistic philosophy of the unbeliever. What a difference it made to my own father! What a difference it made to his family and friends who knew now that he was not dead, but was experiencing real life -- life eternal! All of this renewed my strength to continue on that road leading to Mexico, even though at times, it was a difficult and uncertain one.

"After resigning that last full-time church to return to our seminary studies, we had to rely even more on our faith, for during that time, we had no fixed income with which to pay our seminary expenses. Pulpit committees from various churches approached us with offers to serve in various staff positions, but when we explained that we expected to be in the states only a few months, no one wanted to call us for such a short time. There were occasional opportunities for me to supply-preach, and as wonderful as that was, the travel expenses to get to and from the church left little money from the love offering.

"I remember one weekend when a church gave me a fifty dollar offering for supplying their pulpit. From that, we had to pay tuition and rent, saving only the tithe and enough to provide my food for the following Friday when I left to preach again. Jewell and the baby also had to eat. I was scheduled to preach again the following weekend, but I got sick on Friday and couldn't even get out of bed that weekend. By Saturday night, all of our food was gone. For Sunday morning breakfast, our kitchen cabinet shelf contained only one can of beets someone had given us and the only money we had left was the five dollars we had faithfully put away for that week's tithe. Jewell asked me, 'Orvil, shall I take the tithe to church?'

"Yes, take it, or we will be tempted to spend it on something else."

"She couldn't attend Travis Avenue Church where we belonged, because she didn't have extra money for the bus-fare, so with the baby in her arms, walked to a church nearer the seminary. As I lay alone in that sickbed at home, I prayed that somehow we might have food to eat and that somehow we might be able to continue in school. That very morning, our apartment owner came by to see how I was recuperating from my illness. He also dropped off some mail from the day before. In that mail was a letter from a Mr. O.D. Cumbie, who had been a deacon in the church at Countyline during my pastorate there. Mr. Cumbie had been transferred to Illinois, and we had not heard from him in over two years. The letter read in part: 'Orvil, I have just received my dividend check of one hundred dollars for this quarter, and God has put in my heart the desire to send you half of it. Please find enclosed a check for $50.' The check was dated three days before. On the day the check was written, no one knew how desperately we needed money, especially not Mr. Cumbie. However God knew, and He was merely keeping a promise He made in Isaiah 65:24, when he said, "Before they call, I will answer; and while they are yet speaking, I will hear." I never forgot the wonderful lesson God re-taught me during that time!

"The road leading to Mexico was becoming more apparent to me during those final months in the seminary. As I approached graduation, a famous New York mission leader contacted Dr. R. Lee Scarborough, then President of the Seminary, but more than that, a man whose entire life was directed toward missions and evangelism, about the possibility of his encouraging me to go to New York to work with their mission. Everyone, including Dr. Scarborough, knew I had strong convictions about going to Mexico as a missionary, but Dr. Scarborough agreed to at least present the New York mission as a possibility. He tried to say all the right words to me at exactly the right moment."

"You know son, many of the young people so near to graduation have no idea how they will use their education or their learning, or how they're going to follow God's leading in their lives after they leave here. In your case, I have a personal interest in you. I know that you have some very dear plans. I'm very aware of the strong convictions you hold about serving the Lord as a missionary in Mexico. I'm proud of you for wanting to serve the Lord as part of an active mission field. But son, do you know that you don't need to go all the way to Mexico in order to find an active mission field full of lost people? Why, just across our own country, in New York City, there is a mission already established, and they are looking for someone just like you to coordinate their ministries. You'll likely find everything you're looking for right there. There will be people with whom you can work and minister, and many of them will even be of Mexican descent."

"I listened as patiently as I could, then as politely as I could, I responded to Dr. Scarborough by saying, 'As grateful as I am for your personal interest in me, and as concerned as I am for the people in that mission in New York City, I have already accepted the Lord's Call to follow Him and to serve Him in the country of Mexico, therefore I am not at all interested in any man's call to New York City.' And that was the end of that discussion. I was already deeply committed to what I later wrote down as a 'Three Dimension Vision' - - suggested by Isaiah 6. Alma, find Don that stack of poems I've written over the years. Look for the one entitled 'Three Dimension Vision.' "

"I've got it right here, Orvil. I'm glad you looked it up last week, or I'd never have found it in that jumble of papers in your workroom." She handed the sheet of paper full of words to Orvil, saying, "Do you want me to read it, or would you like to?"

"Just let Don and Kay read it. And while they're doing so, could you get me a glass of water?" He handed Don the paper, one of many from the stack of hand-written poems in the folder. He and Kay read it aloud, while Orvil mouthed the words between sips from the glass of water he held in his knarled hands.

> *Give me, O Lord, an upward look,*
> *To know God's might and purity,*
> *Fill thou my heart to its last nook,*
> *Until I am possessed of thee.*
>
> *Give me, I pray, an inward look,*
> *That I may see my sin and shame*
> *As pictured in Thy Holy Book:*
> *And make thy grace my only claim.*
>
> *Give me an outward look, that I*
> *May see the world's compelling need.*
> *Oh, let me ever hear the cry*
> *Of dying men who for life plead!*
>
> *Help me to hear thy order, "Go!"*
> *And hear the lost world's plaintive, "Come!"*
> *Help me to feel their helpless woe:*
> *And by thy grace deliver some.*

At the end of the poem, Orvil's head was resting on the back of his recliner, his eyes closed. "Is he asleep, Alma?"

"No, Don, I think he's just resting."

With a strong voice, Orvil spoke. "I'm not asleep. And I'm not resting either. I'm just enjoying hearing someone else read my poems, a special privilege I don't often have."

"Would you like to stop for a while, Orvil?"

"In just a minute. I'm almost finished with this part. It wasn't long before I graduated from Southwestern Baptist Theological Seminary, and Jewel and I were appointed as missionaries to Mexico. We'd soon be off to Mexico City to begin training for a lifetime of work in our soon-to-be adopted country of Mexico."

CHAPTER 4

THE FOREIGN MISSIONARIES

They decided to have another session after lunch. Don and Kay grabbed some fast food before going back to their motel so Don could review some of the material he'd been writing down for the past couple of days. Orvil and Alma were just getting up from their afternoon siesta when they arrived back at their house. They tried to insist that the next session could wait until tomorrow, but Orvil would have none of it.

"I'm glad to hear that Orvil, because you left me curious about the details surrounding your going as missionaries to Mexico."

"Let's all have some lemonade to start with"

"No thanks, Alma. You, Don, and Kay can have some if you'd like, but as I said before, I can only do one thing at a time, and I certainly can't talk and drink lemonade at the same time." And he was all ready to talk. And they were ready to listen. So Orvil talked, while the others enjoyed ice-cold lemonade.

"On Nov. 26, 1938, Jewell and two-year-old Roderick and I embarked for Southern Baptist's nearest Foreign Mission Field. We set sail from Oklahoma City headed toward Ft. Worth in a new Plymouth automobile that the Oklahoma W.M.U. had given us as a going-away mission gift. Two days later, we crossed the U.S.-Mexico border and became foreigners. I knew something about how the American boy felt when he wrote his mother from a foreign country, 'Ma, just imagine, all the people here are foreigners, but me!'

"When we arrived on the outskirts of Mexico City, there were guide services everywhere, people hiring themselves out to help visitors find their way into the city. Because we wanted to look for a house in a particular area, we already knew the general area where we wanted to stay for a few days, so we hired a guide to locate a hotel for us in that specific area. The next day, the same guide showed up at our hotel inquiring about the possibility of driving us to the center of town for a tour. On the way to town, he seemed to be taking a route that took many unnecessary left and right turns. I thought he was trying to make it seem so complicated that we would have to hire him to drive us every place, so I assured him that we now knew how to get back to the hotel on our own. The next day, we rented a small house belonging to a French widow and her daughter, who treated us as though we were part of their very own family.

"We entered the International Summer School of the School of Philosophy and Letters of the National

University in July of 1939. Classes in most of the schools in Mexico City began in February and November, and had vacation months in December and January. We attended both the International Summer School and the regular sessions of the University for the remainder of 1939, and all of the school year of 1940.

"We thought at first we might have to remain in Mexico on student permits for five years in order to receive our permanent permits to stay in the country. My plan was to do as much mission work as possible and go to school on the side. All class work was finished for the Master of Arts and Letters degree and the subject for my thesis had been approved. Suddenly, what had seemed impossible became a reality. I was given a permit to stay as Representative of Southern Baptists in Mexico. Until that time, no other missionary of any denomination had ever received such a permit. As providence would have it, I had become friends with the American Ambassador, Mr. Josephus Daniels, who was a good friend and college-mate of Dr. Maddry, executive-director of the Foreign Mission Board. The Ambassador gave me a letter addressed to the head of the Department of Government of Mexico saying in part, 'I know this man and the people he represents, and I will be responsable for him in every way.'

"With that letter, I was immediately received by

the head of the proper committee of the Government, himself a member of the President's Cabinet. I also had a letter in Spanish telling him exactly what my work would be. As I handed the letter to the official, I said to him, 'Señor Aleman, I know the laws about religious work in your country. I have told you in the letter everything that I want to do. You may allow me to stay, or you may run me out of the country, but I am not hiding anything from you.'

"Señor Aleman read the letter, and said, 'Mr. Reid, we are going to give you a temporary permit to stay in Mexico.' And they did. But it had to be renewed each year for four more years before it became permanent. Some years later, this same Mr. Miguel Aleman became the President of Mexico. While he was President, I had the honor of making two visits to his mother's home. She was a Christian, and a member of the Methodist church. She spent almost an hour talking with me about some of the problems that were troubling her. She asked me for copies of some of the books and booklets I had written against alcohol abuse. I promptly sent them to her, as well as a supply of all the anti-alcohol literature, and some of the evangelistic plays. She told me she gave them to her family and friends.

"As soon as Jewell and I could, we joined the First Baptist Church of Mexico City, where Dr.

Alejandro Treviño Ojeda was our pastor. The Mexican people received us with open hearts and arms. There was no language school to which the Mission Board sent its missionaries in those days; neither did new missionaries have any kind of orientation before arriving. With our small language-learning allowance, we hired one of our fellow church members, a student at the University, to tutor us at our house for an hour a day, four days a week. She was younger than we were, so was hesitant to correct us. Someone told me that one has to make a million mistakes before learning a language. I decided to make all my mistakes as soon as I could! I pestered everyone who would listen to me and talk Spanish with me. I listened to Spanish-language radio stations, struggling to understand all I could. It seemed to me that no one spoke slowly. Everyone spoke as fast as lightening. Sometimes I would go to a park, and find someone with whom I could practice my Spanish. The only problem was that many of the people knew a little English better than I knew a little Spanish, and the minute they learned I spoke English, they'd begin to use their English, for they did not want to miss an opportunity to practice their other language.

"It was while I was a student in the Mexican National University that I helped to organize the first and only Baptist Student Union in Mexico at that time. In

1939, the small group of university students who attended First Baptist Church of Mexico City became the nucleus around which we organized this Mexican BSU, loosely structured after the ones I had known in the U.S. A larger group was composed of many students of several other Christian denominations as well as students who had no religious or denominational affiliation. We called ourselves the Christian Philosophy Study Club. The first point in our constitution was this statement: Our purpose is to study the philosophy of the Christian religion as taught by Christ and his apostles in the New Testament. The Christian Philosophy Study Club was really just another name for a Bible Study Club, but calling it that made a difference, for it would have been impossible to enlist some of the students for a Bible Study Club. The so-called 'freethinkers' were impressed by the word 'philosophy', and the Christian Philosophy Study Club often had more than a hundred students in attendance at their meetings.

"I met many freethinkers in that large group of students, whom I considered to be vain and prideful, and who considered themselves to be wise. That's one of the things that prompted me to think and write about 'The Self-Made Man.' Alma, pull that one out of the folder and give it to them to read."

The vain man speaks:
Am I my brother's keeper? Why? Nobody cares for

57

me:
I fight my battles all alone, whatever they may be.
I pride myself upon the fact that I'm a self-made man:
That I am debtor to someone I cannot understand.

The wise man speaks:
When you were born, who cared for you?
Who gave you food and drink?
Had no one cared where would you be?
When have you stopped to think?

Then, as a child in home and school,
While playing, or in church,
Had you no family? Teachers? Friends?
Think! And your memory search.

Were you in youth so strong and wise
You needed none to guide?
When sickness, pain, and sorrow came,
Was no one at your side?

And now that you're a full-grown man,
I think you must agree
That many daily do their part
In serving you and me.

The things we eat and drink and wear
And much we see and hear
That makes our living worth the while
Have cost somebody dear.

All that we have, all that we are,
We owe to some kind hand:
Don't be deceived by selfish myths,
There is no self-made man.

"I wrote many different things during that time. In fact, I've always written poems and essays, but the

58

fact that I encountered so many difficulties in my personal struggle on the road that led me from atheism to Christianity contributed to another writing called 'Faith Conquers Doubt'. After all, I knew some of this from firsthand experience. "

> *What's a life without a purpose?*
> *What's a game without a goal?*
> *What's in life that's worth the struggle*
> *If there is no living soul?*
>
> *Dark, how dark the future beckons,*
> *Vain and empty is the life*
> *When there is no faith to anchor*
> *In the seething sea of strife.*
>
> *If there is no God in heaven,*
> *If this life must be the last,*
> *In despair I wait the moment*
> *When these fleeting hours shall pass.*
>
> *In vain I sat alone and wrestled*
> *With the doubts that tore my soul.*
> *Helpless as a man who's sinking*
> *In the water, dark and cold.*
>
> *My heart so empty, dreading, longing,*
> *Weighted down with all my fears,*
> *Though I laughed when Christians counseled,*
> *I was smiling through my tears.*
>
> *When the hour was at its darkest*
> *I heard a loving, still small voice:*
> *"Come to Christ for Life Abundant.*
> *Leave your doubts, make Him your choice."*
>
> *Out of darkness came a glimmer,*
> *Faith had found a ray of light*

Which burst forth in heaven's splendor.
I, once blind, had found my sight!

Alma was filling everyone's lemonade glass again, when she reminded Orvil to "tell them about that leper colony on the outskirts of
 Mexico City."

"Oh yes, I couldn't forget that. Twenty miles east of Mexico City there was a Federal Leper Colony, built behind high walls to prevent the lepers from leaving the colony. I helped to organize a bible study and mission there, conducting services in a small room on the grounds every other weekend. Men, women and children all lived in the leper colony, and many of them attended the services from time to time. Some were badly mutilated by their disease, while others seemed outwardly perfectly normal. Some lived with only stubs of arms or legs because the disease had taken it's terrible toll on their bodies. Leprosy had attacked the vocal cords of one man until he could hardly speak. He was one of the men who ultimately made a profession of faith, and regularly attended our services. One day he said, 'Brother Reid, I may not be here when you come back next time. I feel that my days on earth are about to end. I would like for you to baptize me.'

"I tried to explain that it was officially against Mexican law to baptize anyone outside of a church

60

building, and obviously the leper could not get out of the colony to go to a church. I tried to assure him that I would be willing to even break the law by baptizing him it if were necessary to his salvation, but it was not. I told him I would even be willing to risk the physical contact with leprosy. The leper answered me by saying, 'I know that baptism does not save, and that Christ has already saved me. I just do not want to go meet my Lord without having done all He asks me to do.'

"All the reassurance I could give him was to say, 'There is no doubt Christ is more pleased with your deep desire to be baptized than He is with some people who go through the act of baptism so lightly that they do not really take seriously what it means.'

"That was the last conversation we ever had, for when we returned to the leper colony two weeks later, he had already gone on to his heavenly home. I could not help but wonder how the Lord had received Him, and how He had assured Him that it was all alright now, even without his having been baptized."

As Orvil talked that afternoon, it was apparent that it had been his commitment to the Lord's Call that had strengthened him to have that upward, inward, outward look. It was following the Lord's Command that had led him to the Mexican National University and to the foundation of the Christian Philosophy Study

Club. It was because Orvil knew firsthand how faith conquered doubt that he had become even more effective in leading others to take their own step of faith. Even though the well-meaning president of Orvil's seminary thought he was saying all the right words, how wonderful that Orvil Wilson Reid was one young pastor who was not tempted to respond when he had heard the words 'You'll likely find everything you are looking for in New York City.' The World of Foreign Missions would have missed an opportunity to have an Orvil Reid as part of its missionary force. And that would have been a greater loss than anyone can imagine.

Before leaving the Reid home that afternoon, Orvil gave Don and Kay a stack of papers and newsletters and poems to read, with full permission to incorporate any of them in the writing and telling of his story. From the beginning of their ministry in Mexico, the Reids wrote and sent their own personal newsletter, YOUR MEXICAN VISITOR. From the one dated May 15, 1939, one can feel much of the urgency they felt:

"Just a word from Beautiful Mexico, the land of contrasts. Every day, every place and even every person is an adventure and challenges the interest. After being here almost six months our hearts are filled with gratitude that God has led us to this great land of urgent need yet with such challenging opportunities. The passion of our hearts is to give the best we have by the help of God in His service in Mexico. We feel that we now understand, at least in part the prayer of John Knox,

'Lord, give me Scotland or I die!'

"Many times we blush with shame when we think of the billions of dollars and the thousands of lives that our native land has given to exploit the material wealth of Mexico, yet has given so little in the interest of the millions of eternal souls who have groped in spiritual darkness through the centuries, darkness as dense as that which envelopes the silver and oil hidden in the bowels of the earth."

CHAPTER 5

THE LONELY YEARS

At 9:30 A.M. the following day, Alma met Don and Kay at the front door with the news that Orvil had gotten up sick in the night.

"I'm sorry, Alma. I'm sure he's tired from our days of talking, taking notes, and recording his story."

"Oh no, Don, it's not that. Before he went to sleep last night, he kept talking about how special it was to be able to relive all this by telling it to you. He thinks its wonderful that you're interested enough to try to put it into a book. Oh no, you've not made him sick. Its something else altogether. Why all of this has made his week a very special one."

"In spite of the reason, Alma, let us go on back to our motel this morning. We'll continue our conversations at another time."

"I wouldn't hear of it. If you'll allow me, I can continue the story where he left off yesterday. As a matter of fact, it may be easier for me to tell you this part of his story than it would be for him."

"That would be fine, Alma, but we don't want to keep you from taking care of Orvil."

"Oh, Orvil will be fine. Come on in, sit down, I have some water on for some hot tea. You do drink tea, don't you? Or would you prefer coffee? I have some instant we can use with the same hot water."

"Tea will be fine."

"Just let me get the cups, then we'll begin."

Don and Kay sat in their usual places opposite the TV table where Alma had set the teacups. She began to talk, as she waited for the water to boil.

"Orvil and Jewell lived and worked believing that verse of scripture which says, 'For we are laborers together with God.' There were times when they only had each other and the Lord and their fellow believers in the organizations and churches with whom to labor. During the early years there were no other active missionaries living in Mexico to help with the ministry. There were three other couples involved in the work, but they all lived near the border in Texas, and all were near the age of retirement. It was a blessing of the Lord that five new missionaries of the next generation of workers were in Mexico studying Spanish. However, of these five active missionaries, three left to work in the seminary in El Paso at the completion of their language studies, and shortly thereafter resigned.

"Those were lonely times for Orvil and Jewell, but it was even worse for their son Roderick, especially when a terrible tragedy happened in his family when he was only four years old. Jewell awoke one night with frightening abdominal pains. Orvil desperately tried to get someone who could recommend a doctor. Finally, a person who worked at the American Consulate told him of a doctor other Americans used, but he did not know the doctor well enough to recommend him. Orvil called him anyway, and Jewell was transported to the hospital in an ambulance. They operated the next day for what the doctor thought was acute appendicitis, but found the problem to be a tubal pregnancy. Her heart was very weak, and she needed an immediate blood transfusion. Since Orvil's blood type was not what she needed, he called First Baptist Church, and some of the young people there gladly donated blood. After the transfusion, Jewell said to Orvil, 'Now we truly have Mexican blood in our family.'

"The day following the transfusion, the doctor informed Orvil that Jewell's condition had deteriorated even more. Her heart was growing weaker, in addition to complicating circulatory problems. They were afraid she wouldn't live much longer. As she was still fully conscious, the doctor suggested that if there were any special decisions they needed to make together, they needed to make them soon. Orvil knew that the very next month they were already scheduled to move to Guadalajara, where his mission work would be to supervise the field work for several states. There was a need to talk about some things, even if it were a difficult time. So he went in.

"Did I give you the copy of THE MEXICAN VISITOR where Orvil told about it all in his own dramatic and emotion-filled words? If not, look in the folder over there, while I get the water for the tea. I'm sure it's boiling by now."

They found the Feb. 20, 1941 copy of his newsletter and read it while Alma prepared the tea in the kitchen.

"It seems like an eternity since we sent out the last newsletter to our friends. That letter was signed 'Mr. and Mrs. Orvil W. Reid and Roderick;' this one I sign alone. God in His infinite wisdom has seen fit to call Jewell to be with Him. Roderick is with his aunt, Wynona Nelson at Jay, Oklahoma. He has a lovely place to stay and they are wonderful Christians. Roderick loves her and her husband and they love him. That was the arrangement Jewell suggested just before she went to rest.

"My mind is too small to understand the Why of things. She had made so many sacrifices, working her way through high school, college and seminary, and had studied hard here to learn the language, both at the National University and in her private classes. She was happier in the last six months than she had ever been in her life. Her health seemingly was good, and she had just begun venturing out, teaching a Sunday School class, talking to Women's Missionary Unions, and had just been elected vice-president of the WMU of the Central Association. At the time she took sick, we had just finished our final exams at the University, and were working in perhaps the largest Vacation Bible School in the history of Mexican Baptists. At least it was the largest held in the First Church of Mexico City.

"On Dec. 1, we rushed her to the American

67

hospital for an emergency operation. Monday morning we gave her a blood transfusion, and the chief surgeon operated. Thursday her heart began to fail; another transfusion and Friday at 8 PM, after we had talked some about the future of Roderick, she said, 'I have known since last night that it was my heart, and that I could not get well, but I have prayed it through and everything is alright. I'm very tired and want to go to rest.' Roderick and I kissed her goodbye 'until morning' and without a struggle she went to sleep. I know that I shall see her in the morning, but the night seems so very long."

As Orvil's elderly Mother and Jewell's mother were both in poor health, they had decided he would take their son, Roderick to live with his Aunt Wynona Starr Nelson, a public school teacher and a wonderful Christian. She was married, but had no children of her own. Orvil continued to talk about that decision in this Feb. 20 newsletter.

"My hardest battle was to be willing to part with my little boy who was five this month. To give them both up at once is hard. Some relatives and friends thought I should settle down and pastor in the states, so I could make a home for my son, my mother, and my seven-year-old brother. It was tempting, because I wanted to be with my boy to teach him, and to win him to the Lord at the earliest possible hour. Then there came to my mind this thought, 'On Whom must you depend for the salvation of your son?' My mind answered back, 'Without God, I am helpless.' 'Would you have faith to ask God to save your boy if you were not willing to leave him and to go back to take the message of salvation and missions to boys and girls who have never heard that God loves one of those under-privileged boys and girls as much as He does your own child?'

68

Just as they finished reading this excerpt, Orvil sauntered down the hall. Alma was just coming in with the hot tea. Everyone greeted everyone, and Kay asked, "So how are you feeling?

"Oh, much better. I think it was just something I ate. How's my life going along now? Where are you in the story?"

"We're sort of at a touching part, my friend. Alma has told us all about Jewell's death, and your decision to let your son go back to Oklahoma to live. But there's no reason for you to have to talk today. Let's pick it up another time."

"No, it's alright. It doesn't bother me to talk about it...now. But I still remember how alone I felt the night Jewell died. I know I was never really alone, for the Lord was with me, but I guess we all have times when He seems so far away from us. Of course, I was also surrounded by my wonderful Mexican brothers and sisters. Even my own flesh and blood could not have done more to support me with their prayers and love than they did. But I couldn't get away from feeling like the world had fallen in on me and was crushing the life right out of me. I tried to remember all the comforting songs and scriptures that might help me. Two of the hymns and one particular verse of scripture came to my burdened

69

mind and a sense of peace began to creep over my grieving heart. The scripture verse was 'My grace is sufficient for thee.' B.B. McKinney's song with that same title, as well as his other song, 'No Never Alone' were of great consolation to me."

Orvil had been standing since he came into the room a few minutes ago. Now, he found his place in his favorite easy chair, as he continued to talk. "Jewell's parents wanted her to be buried in their Starr Community cemetery back in Oklahoma. There were many things that had to be arranged with the Mexican immigration and health authorities. It was almost a week later, before Roderick and I boarded the train bound for the US-Mexican border at Laredo, where just two years before we had all entered Mexico, so thrilled and happy to be coming into the country where Jewell and I had felt the Lord wanted us to invest the rest of our lives.

"In all the last-minute plans, I had forgotten to exchange any money. We had no dollars and the train was scheduled to arrive at the border about midnight and there would be no place to exchange pesos for dollars at that hour. The train had a half-hour stop as it passed through Saltillo, so Roderick and I took a taxi into town to attempt to find a place that would exchange some pesos for dollars. It took more time than it should have and we got back to the station as the train was pulling out of sight. Jewell's body was in the baggage coach, and all our travel baggage was on that train, including all the immigration papers. There would not be another train through there for another twenty-four hours, and in those days, no buses had Saltillo on their route. The taxi driver knew the train had a five-minute stop a little further up the road. If we were willing to pay him, he would try to make it. We had no choice. I had to use some of those very dollars that were going to be so essential when we arrived at the border in order to pay him to catch the train...again!

"As hard as it was to take Roderick back to live in Oklahoma, I knew I had to do it, for I felt I had to continue to follow the Lord's Call to Mexico. But oh, how I missed Roderick. I wrote him letters and I wrote him poems, like the one called 'To My Son.'

> *Nobody knows how I love you,*
> *Nobody knows but God.*
> *Nobody knows the heartache,*
> *Who never the path has trod.*
>
> *Nobody knows the longing,*
> *The ache of living apart.*
> *Nobody knows how empty*
> *Your absence has left my heart.*
>
> *Nobody? Yes, there's Someone*
> *Who gave up His Son for me.*
> *He knows all the pain and the heartache,*
> *He suffered it all for me.*

"So I continued the work in Mexico alone. It had never been an easy work, but it was even less so now. I naturally found myself thinking much about my son, living with his Aunt back in Oklahoma. Many of my thoughts came out in the form of poems, like this one addressed 'To Roderick.'

When you're rising in the morning,
When you're working, or at play,
When you're fading into dreamland
After you have knelt to pray,
Just remember that I love you --
Love you more than tongue can tell,
And my every thought and prayer
Is that God may keep you well.
May He keep you sweet and happy,
Just as God would have you be.
Lord, may heaven's guardian angel
Keep my darling boy for me.

"It went without saying that memories of Jewell Starr also filled many of my waking thoughts. Even though she was not there to help me in the work, not a day passed that I didn't feel her influence would live forever, because of her complete dedication to the Lord and His work in Mexico. To help me through the lonely days, I often poured those feelings into my writings too. One of them was simply titled, 'Missing You.' "

The house is so large without you, my dear.
How vacant and empty it seems.
I catch myself listening your voice to hear,
I see you in real and daydreams.

I miss your laughter and your soft, sweet song,
I miss the bright warmth of your smile.
In such a short time the days have grown long,
And the house seems cold all the while.

Your absence is felt in a thousand ways --
Without you, there's so much I miss.
Each chore I attempt keeps singing your praise,
Perhaps I miss more your sweet kiss.

We miss the water when the well is dry,
Food is missed when the shelf is bare.
And you've been missed most since we said goodbye,
To see you real soon is my prayer!

What would I have done had you never been mine?
Had I walked life's journey alone?
How thankful I am that Mercy Divine
Crowned my life and made you my own!

"I already know what happened next. You folks will just have to wait until at least this afternoon. Hey Alma, what's for lunch? I awoke as hungry as a bear after a winter's hibernation."

CHAPTER 6

THE CORRESPONDENT

Before leaving yesterday's session, Don and Kay told the Reids they'd arrive the next day with a take-in breakfast. They had found a bakery that made *pan dulce*, that delicious sweet bread so popular in Mexico. When they got there with their array of fruit and *pan dulce*, Orvil was already up and about, no worse for the wear from his bad day yesterday, and Alma already had the coffee pot going. She was all smiles as she got everything set out on the table. As she was matching the right cups with the right saucers, she admitted, "I'm always glad to get to this part of Orvil's story, for this is where I come into his life." Her smile broadened when she saw the *pan dulce*. "Orvil, look what they brought us," she said, as she proudly held up a piece of the Mexican pastry for him to see.

They weren't but a few delicious bites into the pastry, when Orvil began talking about what happened next. "Wait," Don said, "I don't even have my tape recorder plugged in yet." He paused long enough to finish his piece of bread in one large bite, and to gulp down a tall glass of orange juice. That gave Don time to get his tape recorder and legal pad in place before Orvil was off and running.

"After I left Roderick in Oklahoma, I was on my way back to Mexico following Jewell's burial, when I was asked to speak at Southwestern Seminary's Chapel Service. I had no idea what I was going to say. I simply wanted my talk to leave an impact on the life of at least one of the students in chapel that day. My now good friend, James Crane, was a young seminarian, who, although directly involved in home missions as the student pastor of a small Mexican church, had not heard the clear call to Foreign Missions at that time. He was the type who always liked going to Mission Chapels though, for he was always interested in seeing those whom God was going to call out to the Mission Fields of the world."

As badly as Don hated to interrupt Orvil, he needed to tell him something. "We visited with the Cranes at their little retirement home on the other side of the Seminary yesterday afternoon. He told me something about the day you spoke in chapel. He remembers at least two important things you had to say -- you told them about the death of your wife, and about your bringing your young son back to the states, and about the pain you felt from having to leave him for a time. That moved him. He was also deeply impressed when you told them how fortunate your son was to have family folks and friends who would help take care of him. You were sure they would tell him about Jesus when he was old enough to understand it all. But you reminded them, that in Mexico there were hundreds of boys and girls who had no one to love them or tell them about the love of Jesus. That's why you had to go back and do your part. So you challenged some of those students to give their lives to the Lord in full-time mission service too. The other thing you did, according to James Crane, was ask anyone interested in receiving your newsletter to give you their name and address. James remembers doing that, and he soon began receiving copies of your personal newsletter, YOUR MEXICAN VISITOR. He says these were pivotal days in his life. He soon began to feel a personal involvement in intercessory prayer for you and the work in Mexico. He looks back to those specific days as the beginning of his deep interest in Mexico, and he credits you with that intercessory prayer involvement that ultimately led to his specific commitment to foreign missions."

As Alma began to clear the table, she said, "James Crane didn't know that that in a few years, he and his wife Edith, whom he married a few years later, would become some of our best friends as we served the Lord alongside each other on that Mexico Mission Field. Can I tell the next part Orvil? After all, I can tell it from a more personal viewpoint than you can."

"Of course, Alma, just don't get carried away with it."

"It may not have been significant at that particular time in Orvil's life, but I was one of those students who DIDN'T hear him speak that day at Southwestern Seminary Chapel. I was just a plain and simple girl, Alma Ervin, a student from Tennessee, who had received her B.A. degree from Union University in 1939, and was now attending Southwestern. To help with expenses, I was working as the secretary for Christian ethics professor, Dr. T.B. Maston. The secretaries almost always talked about that day's chapel speaker after returning to work. It didn't take but moments for those other girls to begin to talk to me about the man who had spoken in chapel that day. I didn't have the opportunity to tell them that I wasn't even there.

"One gushed, 'Oh Alma, what did you think? Wasn't he one of the most inspirational speakers we've heard in a long time?' "

Another secretary rolled her fluttering eyes back, as she said, "Alma, I could have just bawled when he talked about the death of his wife, and how he had to bring his small son back to the states to live. What did you think?"

"I think you girls didn't have all the work to do that I did, or you'd have missed chapel today too!"

"Oh, poor dear, you didn't even get to go? Oh Alma, let me tell you -- he was so tall. And so strong. And having just lost his wife and all...and being a missionary...and...and..."

"And I got his address. He asked any of us to write him in order to receive his missionary newsletter. I certainly want to. Would you like to have it Alma?"

"For some reason, " Alma said almost nonchalantly, "I never got that address, and I never gave that tall, widowed missionary chapel speaker a second thought. Not at that time at least! I had felt many times during my seminary days that the Lord just might be calling me as a missionary, but I wasn't really sure, so I resigned myself to serving as a Director of Church Education, hoping it might be nearly as fulfilling.

"Following my graduation from Southwestern in 1941, Dr. Maston recommended me for a job in the Church Administration Department of the Baptist Sunday School Board in Nashville. It was an excellent opportunity for me to learn from others, while at the same time working as editorial assistant of The Sunday School Builder magazine. I got to travel all over the country leading Study Courses as a representative of the Sunday School Board. One summer while at Ridgecrest

Baptist Assembly in North Carolina, I re-dedicated myself to the Lord's Call and re-committed my life to Foreign Missions. I told him again I would go wherever He wanted me to go. I was even willing to go as a single missionary if that were part of His total design and purpose for my life. From that point on, I at least felt more available to be used by Him in Mission Service than I had before. Little did I know the mysterious workings God was going to perform in my life.

"The next year, the Southern Baptist Convention was meeting in San Antonio, Texas, and I was sent there to work in the products booth of the Sunday School Board. As much as I enjoyed the editing, the representation of the Board, and the traveling, I now genuinely felt that all of that was only preparation for something else the Lord wanted me to do in my life. In San Antonio, many people came by the booth to talk and receive information about the latest products and publications. One of those people was missionary Orvil Reid. We began to talk. As naturally it would, the conversation turned toward the mission field, and I told him of my interest in serving there someday. He told me about the work in Mexico. And about his first wife. And her death. And his son. His story and the way he told it touched me in a special way, and I realized there were tears running down my cheeks as I stood there listening to him. As I tried to casually wipe them away, I remembered some of the things those office secretaries had said about Orvil when he spoke in Southwestern Seminary chapel two years before. I couldn't help but think that perhaps they were right. He was tall. And he was dynamic. And he was a widower. And he was dedicated to missions. And right then, he was standing there face to face with me, telling me all about himself. He told me how he wouldn't even have been in San Antonio had he not come there to see his mother and his son who were attending the Convention from Oklahoma.

"When the convention was over, Orvil returned to Mexico, where he began to write me. Except for what he had told me that day, and what I remembered about him from friends at Seminary, I really knew nothing more about him. That was fine, for though we had passed some pleasant moments in conversation at the convention booth in San Antonio, and even though my emotions had been touched by what he had said, I still didn't really find myself interested in him at all. But he continued to write. And he wrote some more. I finally wrote him back. In the beginning, it was more from a sense of politeness than anything else. Kay, get that folder I laid out on that box at the end of the sofa. It's labeled LETTERS. Now read the first part of the one right on top. I was quite formal when I wrote that one."

Kay found the box and began to read. "July 13, 1942. Dear Mr. Reid, Thanks for sending me THE VISITOR. It was very interesting and worth all the time and effort it must have taken. I appreciated too, the note with your words of encouragement, the poem, and the pictures."

Kay looked at Alma, as she said with a wink, "As the letters came and went, Alma, I suspect that something of their content began to change."

"Oh yes, my dear Katie. As I went through a personal disappointment, I shared it with Orvil in the next letter. Let me read you part of the next one, Kay.

Wasn't it awful of me to tell you about my disappointment when I am practically a stranger and you have enough trouble yourself? I was sorry that I mentioned it to you until I received your letter and the poem, and then I was glad that I told you. You helped me so much.' "

"From the size of this letter file, it looks like your correspondence grew, Alma."

"Oh it definitely did, Don. Look at the next one where I told him about my possible missionary appointment."

"I will probably go to Richmond in August and to a language school in the fall, if I pass the examinations. I don't know when I will go, or how it all will work out. But if I don't get through the closed door, I can still stay at home and be happy, as long as I know it is the Lord's will. We are having a great week at

Ridgecrest and a large crowd in spite of traveling conditions. I guess I am having the best time of anybody. Last night when Dr. Maddry spoke and I made my decision public, it was a mountain-top experience for me."

Kay pulled out a letter dated August 23, 1942.

"Here's the one about your trip to Richmond."

"Dear Mr. Reid: When I returned from Richmond, I found your letter here. I don't know whether your experience at Richmond was similar to ours or not. It was a very trying week for all of us--the long hours of waiting, the slow procedure, and the suspense. We arrived in Richmond on Friday and left Monday. But in spite of all the strain, we had some fun too. I was quite sure that most of us would pass the examination, but three of us did not. And when I say 'three of us' I really mean just that -- I did not pass the physical examination. That seems hard to realize when I feel so well. But because my mother died of tuberculosis and my lungs are weak, the doctor said it would be easy for me to take tuberculosis or some other disease if I had to do the hard work that mission work requires. My own doctor here thinks that I could do the work, but of course he is not the one to decide.
"I won't say that this was not a disappointment, because you know that it was. The disappointment was even greater because the man in charge of Dr. Maddry's office told me that I passed. Then he learned that he had made a mistake.
"One sentence from your letter has meant so much to me, and maybe I mentioned it in my other letter. You said, 'You must always be a missionary.' Those words have gone through my mind so many times, and I know that I will always be a missionary. I'm so thankful that I did get to go to Richmond. Even though I can't understand why the Lord called me and I can't go, still I am so glad that He did call me and I am thankful for

every experience in connection with it.

"I hope this letter won't sound as though I were too much in the valley. There will be other mountaintop experiences. Both the mountaintop and the valley seem to be a part of life. I believe that my faith is greater than ever before and I am just as submissive to the will of God as I was when I answered His call to go to the ends of the earth or wherever He wanted me to go.

"It means so much to me to know that you are praying for me each day. I hope too, that as I pray for you each day, you may be able to feel the added strength and power of the Lord.

"I just can't tell you how much I appreciate your poems. I hope you will send me some more. I had a lot of fun while I was in the hospital in Richmond when I attempted to do a little writing during the hours of waiting. I think I wrote a verse about everything and everybody. Most of them were ludicrous and quite absurd, but there had to be a funny side to relieve the tenseness. I know you have very little time for writing but I think you have what it takes to be a poet or writer. So I think you should keep right on with your writing.

"Did you take the plane to Durango? A plane trip sounds so exciting to me. I hope I can take one sometime. I have been up in a small plane, but have never taken a trip. I hope you got along all right with the Vacation Bible School work, the associational meetings, and so on. It must be awfully hard for the churches to keep going where there are no pastors.

"The work you mentioned in your letter sounds so interesting, and exactly like the type of work I would like to do. But evidently it was not the Lord's will or it would have worked out differently. I hope that the right person may be led to do this work, for the need does seem to be so great. I know how you must feel, with the need so great, the field so big, and the workers so few. The fact that the challenge is so great makes you depend upon the Lord more, I am sure, and at the same time makes your accomplishments greater.

"Don't forget that I am praying for you, and I hope that you will feel free to mention any particular burden or problem. Best of wishes to you. Sincerely, Alma Ervin."

"And at the bottom of that same letter, you added your poem, CONSOLATION, written August 10, 1942, in Tucker Hospital, Richmond, Virginia. Read it to us, Alma."

"I'm not sure I can, but I'll try."

O that awful disappointment
That finally came to me,
After hours and hours of waiting
For the words to set me free.

Four of us were waiting, waiting,
Four now out of the six,
Another long day we waited
For words our life work to fix.

'Tis o'er the hours of waiting --
"Go free patients, go free."
'Tis China's far shore for two of us,
'Tis South America for me."

"Could there be some mistake doctor? --
Those words coming from you.
O tell me again that I passed,
I long so His will to do.

To a foreign land I will go,
It's been my dream so long;
Alas, that dream came tumbling down,
For the report he'd given was wrong.

"I'm sorry," and he was so contrite

84

The report says you did not pass."
Just those words and my world changed
And my heart began to beat so fast.

The tears they fell silent and long
In a very torrent of rain,
And from my heart I could feel
A terrible aching pain.

O God, heal this aching heart
The disappointment is so great.
What can I do now Lord?
Do they also serve who wait?

Came back the answer soft and clear
No waiting, my child, for you.
"I've work for you in the homeland,
Calling for Christians true.

This was all a part of my plan,
I asked that your all you give;
You've given it child, and now
A richer life you'll always live."

Alma quickly left the table. Everyone else just sat there absorbing something of the intensity and emotion of her words. She was only gone a minute before she came right back to the dining room, suggesting, "Let's move back into the living room. We can get these dishes cleaned up later. Maybe Orvil would like to read some of the other letters to you."

"I'll try. After all, they *were* written to me. I don't know whether that news was more disappointing to the two of us than we had hoped or not, but for whatever

85

reason, our writing slacked off for a couple of months. You need to remember, this correspondence was all taking place during the war years, and even though parts of our letters were censored, that did not change the feelings that were growing between us, feelings that were now finding their way into words in our letters. We wrote many letters in the months that followed. As subtle as it was, even the greetings at the beginning of our letters were now much less formal. Let me have that folder, Don." They all waited patiently as he took the folder and shuffled through it until he found the letter he wanted to read.

"Dec. 3, 1942. Dear Orvil, as I sit here in my room writing, I can look out the window and see a deep snow. It snowed nearly all day and it was so beautiful outside I could hardly sit at my desk and work. This is our first snow this season.

"You were right when you said it had been a long time since you had heard from me -- the reason being I had not heard from you in a long time. I did hear from you through the 'Visitor', so perhaps I should have written.

"I read in the 'Visitor' where someone broke a stone over someone's stomach with a sledge hammer, and four men failed to bend a person's leg. Did they do all that to you? I don't blame the children for pledging never to touch alcohol after such a demonstration as that. Be careful with all those stones and sledge hammers -- or maybe you should tell the ones who use them to be careful.

"Thanks for sending me the picture. And I am sending one in exchange as you requested -- even with the smile. I'm sorry I had to be smiling through tears when you saw me last. Anyway, I promise when you see me again, I will be smiling and there will be no tears. I certainly don't feel like crying now and I don't feel any disappointment. I am sure that your prayers have had a great deal to do with my feeling the way I do about it.

"When 'the missionary writes personally' I will write to you again. Sincerely, Alma."

"Here's one I wrote back to her:

12/15/42. Dear Alma: Just arrived in this city a few minutes ago, and found some letters waiting for me. In one of them I found a picture of a young lady about whom I have thought and for whom I have prayed daily for some time. In spite of the fact that I looked real carefully at the smile, I could find no trace of a tear. If the one I saw forcing its way through the tears, like the sun through the clouds, seemed beautiful, this one was more so. You ought to be able to collect with it from Pepsodent! Ha!

"First I looked at the picture and saw you sitting outside with a summer dress on. Then I read the first lines of the letter where you said that you were sitting, writing the letter, and that you could look out at the snow. I looked at the picture and wanted to tell you to put your coat on. As I couldn't do that, I just placed you in my billfold and put you in my pocket and -- sat down on you! That did away with the problem of the cold, and at the same time helped me to 'get back at' a certain little girl who talked about 'the reason being that I had not heard from you for a long time -- when the missionary answers PERSONALLY I will write to you again', etc. etc. However you will note, that in spite of all these extreme measures, I am complying, and writing PERSONALLY and SOON -- even before answering Uncle Charley's letter that came at the same time.

"Really, did you not receive a long personal letter from me about two weeks before getting THE MEXICAN VISITOR? If not, it must have been lost, or

Uncle Sam thought it was about 'secrets of state' or that I was trying to sabotage you. You will not have to worry about my NOT writing, but I fear I may trouble you too much. If I do, you must take the blame. Why? For sending me THAT picture, instead of one not so inviting. Ha! I am writing PERSONALLY, but if you make the fatal mistake to suggest that it also be in longhand, you will repent in sackcloth and ashes, for you would have to call in the neighbors to help you translate it. That would be embarrassing perhaps.

"You asked about the athletic demonstrations. The kids always wonder why my leg doesn't break or why they can't turn me over. It's easy ---shhh, I'll tell you the secret. All you have to do is to just be real stubborn and not bend or turn over. Try it sometime. Ha!

"I'm now in Ciudad Obregon, Sonoro, to give some anti-alcohol conferences. From here I leave for Culiacan, then to Mazatlan, then to Tepic. From there I go to Guadalajara, but will only be there for a few days, as I must go on to Colima. Then I must go to Manzanillo, our southern port. They are almost ready to put the roof on their new church building, and want me to help them for a day or two. After I return to Guadalajara, I will have just three or four days before going to Puebla to help in the 2nd Baptist Encampment. Wish you were here to help us out in the meeting. Perhaps you could not talk, but you could at least bring the smile, *Verdad*? Is it not so?

"I see that this letter is about 90% half nonsense, but after looking at the picture, who wouldn't feel like relaxing, after these weeks of intense work, and smile with you. However you are 'saved by the bell' this time from being bored more, because it is time for me to go to speak in the church. Your letter, and the knowledge that you are praying for me, give me new strength for the task. I do not want to trouble you too much, but you will write when you have time -- if you do not, you are a bad, bad girl. Your friend, Orvil.

"For some apparent reason, Alma began to take an increased interest in Spanish. Listen to what she wrote me in February of 1943.

"Thank you for your book. I think I got more from the illustrations than anything else. I could get the meaning of a few Spanish words, but only enough to make me want to read the other words. The very next day after I received your book, I learned quite by accident that a Spanish class was going to be started right here at the Board by some of the girls. The Spanish book and the Spanish class coming all the same week was rather a coincidence. I decided that since I was surrounded by so much Spanish, I ought to learn what it was all about, so I went to class last night.

"Today I feel that my knowledge of Spanish has greatly increased. Our teacher is very good. He has spent several yeas in South America, in Spain, and in Africa. I really did enjoy the class last night. You should have heard me reading sentences in Spanish and translating them into English. It seems that more people are taking Spanish now. They have three Spanish classes at Watkins Night School here. That is where I finished my high school work. It really is a good school. The girls' club at the YWCA here also has a Spanish class.

"I am leaving in the morning for Oklahoma for a week, to teach a study course there. I hope I won't get too far behind in my Spanish class while I am gone. Maybe soon I can write you a letter in Spanish, but it will be a very short letter, with plenty of errors. I will tell you about Oklahoma when I return, and the letter will be in English. Sincerely, Alma."

"And just a few sentences from her letter of March 4 reveals more than a hint of her growing interest not only in the language I used in Mexico, but in me as well, despite what she had told those secretaries, and despite what she may have been trying to convince herself.

"I was glad to find all the letters that came during my absence. One important letter that I received was yours of course. I am not always so prompt with my letter writing. I usually wait about as long as the other person does about writing. For example, if you were to wait a month before answering my letter, then I would wait about a month before answering yours. Is that the right way to do? If I knew that the person was real busy, I might make an exception in that case.

"I think Oklahoma is a great state, even though it is your native state. The people there were so friendly and it seemed that they couldn't do enough for us -- that seems to be the Oklahoma and Texas spirit.

"I did not know that you are part Indian. I think that is something to be proud of. I can't claim that distinction -- I am just plain Scotch-Irish. Back to the Spanish -- wouldn't I like to have you for my teacher! In spite of the fact that you know more horrible punishments for those who might not know their lessons. And I am quite sure that I won't always know my lesson so well..*hasta luego*.'

"I wasn't the only one, Orvil. It was about this time that you began YOUR letters to me in a slightly different way as well. Note the salutation on this one dated 3/14/43.

Dearest Alma: What a pleasant surprise to receive your letter today. Am glad you liked Oklahoma. Of course they liked you and could not do enough for

90

you. How could they do otherwise....You were mistaken in what you are. You said that 'I am just PLAIN Scotch-Irish'. It may be that you are Scotch-Irish, but the PLAIN doesn't fit you. As I do not know if the Irish or the Scotch dominates, I do not know if I should call you 'My Wild Irish Rose' or 'My Bonnie Lass'.

You have a lot of courage and faith to say that you would like me for a teacher, but of course you were only joking. However you must be careful or your jests might be prophecy. Anyway you could not even begin to want the teacher as much as he would like the job. They tell us that the first need of the teacher is to love the pupil and to have a personal interest in his development. That is the only point where I get 100% plus! However if I had the job, it would cost you a fortune -- lots and lots of pesos each day. (I mean the kind of 'pesos' you spell with a 'b' instead of a 'p'. Now look that up in your dictionary!) It is a very special price and I only make it to you in your character of 'special student'. Lots of love from your 'hypothetical teacher', Orvil."

"You know," Alma laughed, "those '*pesos*' he wanted to spell with a 'b' to receive as payment for teaching me Spanish, came out to be '*besos*', the Spanish word for 'kisses'. I didn't know that at the time, but you'd better believe I looked it up in my dictionary. Our correspondence became quite extensive, and Orvil especially became quite open with the words he wanted me to hear, even if he had to write them to me, instead of saying them to me in person. In this other letter he said, 'How is your Spanish? *Te quiero mucho*. I wonder if you will ever be able to write this Mexican friend those three words and mean every one of them. Just to be

91

mean, I won't translate them.' And he didn't, although I quickly learned they meant 'I love you very much.' He also wrote, 'Don't forget your 'debts' and write soon. When I looked back at the salutation for this letter, I was tempted to erase those words 'Dearest Alma' for fear that you might feel I should not have used them. However we agreed to always be sincere, and I can truly say that, of all the friends I know, the one who holds the largest place in my heart is the one I only remember seen but once. However in that brief moment, as I looked into the windows of her soul, something that I cannot explain seemed to knit my heart to hers. If it is of the Lord, she will be led to feel the same way. If not...I will say it was a dream, and will always be thankful that my life at least was enriched with a real friend.' "

"And part of your response in this letter, dated March 18, 1943 went like this:

"The 'debt' is paid -- for I answered the 'extra' letter even before you asked me to. You wondered if I would ever be able to say *'Te Quiero Mucho'* to my Mexican friend and mean every word. I don't know, but unless I did mean every word, I would never say it. It was quite all right about the salutation, of course. I think you know that you hold just as large a place in my heart as a friend as I do in yours. And for a real friendship I think it should be like that. I must get home for this is my night to go roll bandages for the Red Cross. It sounds easy but it is really hard work because they have to be folded just so-so, and 'roll' is really the wrong term. I don't put 'serious' and 'not serious' after each statement in my letters, but hope you can pick out which is which.

Anyway, I am serious when I say that I appreciate you lots and lots (and if my grammar is not correct, my sentence is). Sincerely, Alma."

"And look at this one. April 21, 1943. Dearest Orvil: Your letter came today, the pictures came day before yesterday. I will have to take your word rather than my own opinion as to whether or not your picture is good. I think it is, but I don't really remember exactly how you look.

"I heard President Avila Camacho of Mexico speak over the radio last night. I am glad they gave us a summary in English of what he said. I don't think I understood four or five words he said in Spanish, and I never did understand all the words in any one sentence. I think he and President Roosevelt both made real good speeches.

"I like the poem you wrote so much--the one you wrote in class. Ordinarily I guess it is not a good idea to do things like that in class, but sometimes--well, I wrote a little rhyme right in one of my Church History Classes at Seminary. You do remember don't you, that some professors are quite famous for 'chasing rabbits' or 'getting off on some long story that is far off the lesson'. When that happens, I find I don't always follow, so one day I had the sudden impulse to write these lines, although I know they are very crudely expressed and the thought itself is not so lofty.

> The long, long hours go rolling by,
>   The rabbits come thick and fast;
> The professor smiles and talks awhile,
>   And finally the minutes pass.
>
> One brother sits a'reading,
>   One sister seems to sigh,
> Some are writing letters,
>   The rabbits go jumping by.

Now we jump to our pencils,
 The rabbits are on the run;
An important fact is bursting forth,
 Don't we Seminary folks have fun?

"Now what do you think about a dignified Seminary student who would write something like that? I never did let my professor read it, I'm afraid he wouldn't have appreciated it. This letter is getting long after all and it is getting late. Love, Alma."

Orvil, who had been listening quietly for a while, spoke now. "So I decided to send Alma a telegram, asking her for some sort of a 'yes or no commitment to a proposal.' Her letter back to me, dated April 24, 1943, read in part:

"You are going to be disappointed when you read this letter, and I am sorry. I thought I would know what to say if I wrote to you today, and I don't. When the telegraph office operator read me your wire over the telephone, I believe I was to wire you if my answer was 'yes'. So I didn't wire you.

"I am right between the 'yes' and the 'no'--and that is a bad place to be. The indecision is not good for me--in fact it is a terrible way to be. And the suspense is bad on you. I wouldn't have it to be like this if there was anything I could do about it, for my own sake, but mostly for yours.

"If I had said 'yes' it would have been at least until fall before I could have been ready. I like your suggestion about the place. And either Guadalajara or Mexico City would have been all right.

"Orvil, I have an idea and I wonder what you think about it. Sometime, could you work in the northern part of Mexico, and then could you come over

94

into Texas for a little while, without asking permission from the Board? Would that be all right with them? And if I were taking my vacation and visiting some friends in Madisonville, could we see each other?

"About Dr. Maddry and the Board -- I don't see any need to be in a hurry about that. After all, the Board could call a special meeting if they wanted to. It has been done. The decision of the Board last summer when I went to Richmond has nothing to do with the answer to the question you asked.

"My pet dream, after the decision of the Board, was that I could save up enough money and when I retired, I would go and do mission work, without the assistance of the Board, and without the assistance of anyone else. Your plans offer an easy solution to my problem. And I have a feeling that the Board at your suggestion would appoint me. Some would-be missionaries and some would-be Mrs. would think it an ideal solution. But I don't. The mission field is not necessary to my happiness, neither is a husband. Some people marry for companionship, and some for other reasons just as crazy. But I wouldn't. The only reason why I would ever marry (and that is the only reason for my not being married now) is that I would have to love the person with all my heart -- not just 'love' but a real deep love. (Every time I think about the censors reading my letters, my face gets red all over. I guess you feel the same way about your letters.)

"That formal question you asked did surprise me. I knew how you felt, and I knew how I felt. But somehow I had the impression that I was supposed to tell you something before you asked that. Didn't you write one time, 'I will not ask you to...until you...' So I thought you would not ask me until I told you whatever it was you wanted me to tell you. I guess it is just as well that you didn't call me by telephone. I couldn't have told you anything anyway.

"Well, at least I am not saying 'no' in this letter. Maybe after you have read this letter you will wish I had.

I may be even too sympathetic at times, but no matter how much I feel for you and think about your needs and the needs in the work--and even though I wish so much that I could have wired you what you wanted me to--still I can't say something I don't feel. And you already know my feelings and all that I have said--that hasn't changed--it just doesn't go far enough. I still think that everything will work out all right and that what's to be, will be. With love, Alma."

"My alternate suggestion that I try to meet Orvil in Texas was obviously a good one, but Orvil convinced me to extend that Texas vacation into Mexico, in order that I could see some of 'his Mexico.' In the weeks that followed, arrangements were made and I took my vacation in order that I could do just that. This sightseeing trip was also going to allow us to be able to finally spend some time together. Orvil proved himself to be the perfect host: he arranged all the details of my trip right down to the perfect places where I would stay, and all the perfect people I would meet and get to know plus the perfect sights to see."

"It was a perfectly wonderful good time for both of us. During that trip, I proposed to Alma, and she said yes. So we became officially engaged, ring and all. On the train trip back from Mexico to the border of Texas, Alma had a scheduled change to make at a certain town to another cross-country train. The train on which she was riding arrived too late to make the connection, so it was necessary for her to stay overnight in a small hotel in that town, while awaiting the next day's train. Speaking hardly any Spanish, she did somehow manage to point to something on the menu that night in order to receive something to eat. The following morning, she learned that the train was not due to arrive until afternoon. She attempted to pass some time having breakfast at the hotel, but again had problems ordering in Spanish. To her good fortune, there was another tourist there who spoke French, which Alma had studied in college, so helped her order a hearty and proper breakfast. Following breakfast, rather than just sit there impatiently waiting, she decided a walk around town would help her pass the time. After walking a while, she realized she was lost, and had no idea where she was, or where the hotel was. Of course, she also had no idea how to ask directions to get back there in order to catch the ongoing train. She was on the verge of desperation, when she encountered some Mennonites who spoke English, and were able to help her get back to a central hotel, hopefully the one where she was staying. It was, and she was grateful to be back in time to catch her train and continue her journey home. On the trip home, she had plenty of time to reflect on how much she had fallen in love with Mexico in such a short time.

"In one of my next letters to Orvil, I told him all about my dream vacation and the plans which were soon to follow."

"June 30, 1943. Dearest Orvil, The people have all been very kind to ask questions about my vacation-- where I went and if I had a good time. When they learn that I went to Texas, they always want to know what part. I am not going to tell them about my plans for September until a short time before then. I have told three or four of my friends but they are not working here at the Board. It is hard enough for me to work as it is and if the people here at the Board start talking about it, there will be no end. There are so many of them here and I couldn't get any work done for showing them my ring and answering questions.

"My trip now is beginning to seem like a dream. For a few days it did seem very real but now it seems more like a dream than anything that actually took place. The plans for September seem just as unreal as the trip or rather they seem like plans that we are making for someone else. I will write the people in Kansas City in a few weeks and tell them why I am not coming there. October is too long for us to wait anyway. We will make it to the last of September or sometime in September. With love, Alma."

"And in this letter of August 12, 1943, I wrote

him:

"If everything is clear, I could come before the FMB October 12-13. And that date is all right, not much later than we had planned. You say it would be nice to publish the news in 'The Visitor' about two weeks before I come. And then suppose I decided not to come? Could you make the correction in the next one? Everybody here at the Board knows about us now, which is fine with me."

Kay, always the romantic, let out a big sigh, as

she said, "Now it was complete. For now you had fallen in love not only with Orvil Reid's Mexico. You had truly fallen in love with Orvil Reid himself, hadn't you Alma?"

CHAPTER 7

THE NEW LOVE

"Let's stop for a coffee-break. All this mushy stuff has dried my mouth out so much that I can hardly talk," Orvil said. Everyone agreed that it was time for a break. Yet, Alma didn't seem to want to stop talking about their love story.

"It didn't take long for us to realize that our enjoyable friendship and constant correspondence had led to our falling deeply in love. Once we were sure that God was involved in our coming together, and we knew it was all right with Him, we felt it was all right for us as well. We also knew it was all right that we wanted to get married. Orvil broke the big news in his next newsletter, which likely came as a big surprise to many of his readers."

"I remember seeing that newsletter in the stack you gave us to read at our motel. I pulled it out, now where did I put it? Here it is," Don said.

"August 20, 1943. Over four months have passed since YOUR MEXICAN VISITOR has knocked at your door. I am so ashamed of myself when I think of your kindness and my neglect...perhaps you may understand better after reading this letter. Beside my regular duties of regular missionary of five states, and being responsable to the Board for four others, since last I wrote, it has been my joy to teach in the Institute for

100

Workers in Saltillo, attend the National Baptist Convention, and the annual meeting of Missionaries in Monterrey.

"The National Convention gave me the responsibility of promotion of evangelism and stewardship throughout the country, and the Young People's Convention asked me to continue as director of publication and distribution of tracts."

Under a heading WHAT GOD HAS JOINED TOGETHER, at the

very end of that four-page newsletter, he included the following:

"It has been almost three years since God called Jewell to be with Him. Since then, I have felt loneliness in my heart that only driving myself almost night and day in the work could keep back. I never dreamed that I would ever be able to love the same way again. However, God knows best for us.

"Since the Southern Baptist Convention in San Antonio, I began writing a young lady, and we found that our friendship had ripened into love before we realized it. She is a mission volunteer, and a graduate of Southwestern. At present, she is an Associate Editor of the Sunday School Builder, helps in secretarial work, and teaches study courses for the Sunday School Board.

"She is fitted for the work here in many ways. Reared an orphan, and working her way through college and seminary, she is trained to endure the hardships of a missionary. Her experience in editorial and Sunday School work will be of great value to the work here. I am thankful for these qualities that can be used for the Lord's Work. However, I am still old-fashioned enough to believe that real matches are made in Heaven, and that a true heart-overflowing love is the best indication of his Will.

"Her name is Miss Alma Ervin of Tennessee. It

means a lot for a girl to leave a good job, with fine cultured companions to come to a foreign field where she will have no English-speaking friends. Pray that I may be able to make her happy, and that the Lord will bless her in His Work here.

"By the way, just in case, please do not send us any wedding presents here. Just send us a big bundle of your love and prayers."

"So I was appointed a missionary of The Foreign Mission Board of the Southern Baptist Convention in October of 1943. Later that same month, I went to Mexico, where I married Orvil Wilson Reid on Oct. 25, 1943, in a civil ceremony attended by the U.S. Consul in Mexico City. The religious ceremony was performed in Mexico City's First Baptist Church. Orvil's friend and language school student Bill Webb performed the ceremony, with his wife Inez serving as my attendant, while Moises Arevelo, who worked with Orvil, was his best man. I stayed in the Webb's home while making the wedding arrangements. They also hosted a reception there following the ceremony.

"We enjoyed an abbreviated honeymoon-trip, because Orvil was concerned that 'all the red tape of getting married' had taken longer than he had planned, and he had not left much money with the cook at the Student Home back in Guadalajara, and the boys and girls there had to eat."

Orvil chimed in saying, "You can tell I had my

priorities in order."

Alma just responded with, "Oh, you!!"

"So with my new bride at my side, we headed back home -- across the country to Guadalajara. In the November 23, 1943 issue of YOUR MEXICAN VISITOR, I informed them that, 'Alma told me to be sure and not say anything about her, but as she is about the biggest news we have in these parts, I guess I will have to start off by not being an obedient husband.' Find the rest of that newsletter for me, Katie. I remember writing something about the wedding, and one of the unusual stops we made on the trip back to Guadalajara."

Kay found it, and read it aloud.

"On the way back, we had a three day honeymoon trip, stopping off at Morelia and Uruapan. We wanted to see the volcano and were surprised to find that three small ones had broken out at the base of the large one. The large one, now over 1,000 feet high, rolls out miles of smoke and leaves all the fire and thunder to the largest of the babies. It is an awe-inspiring sight to see tons of fire-white rocks thrown hundreds of feet into the air, and to hear the constant cracking and thundering as if a dozen large cannons were firing. One can walk a half-mile over the molten lava. You see, the surface cools and hardens, even when it is still red hot underneath."

"That's what every new bride wants on her

103

honeymoon, "Alma laughed, "the threat of the two of you being killed by a fire-spewing volcano. It was OK, but when we got back to Guadalajara, there was a big party arranged by the boys and girls in the student homes. There were games, wedding gifts, and all. I still couldn't speak a word of Spanish and didn't understand it all, but thanks to one of the young men, Jorge Gaspar, I got a welcome in English. Traditional Mexican wedding reception foods were in abundance, and *tamales* and *atole* were enjoyed by all. Even though the boys hated to see Orvil go, they understood why he and his new bride moved to the upstairs apartment of the girls' student home. It didn't seem to matter to Orvil where we lived. He once wrote only of the qualities of 'A Christian Home.' "

Of all wondrous sights I see as I roam,
There's none can equal a sweet Christian home.
No worldly pleasure can bring the true joys
Of one's own companion, one's own girls and boys.

Although there are moments of discord and strife,
The times of forgiveness are sweetening to life.
A hut or a mansion, small difference can make,
When love reigns, and each lives for the other's sake.

"That's beautiful," Kay said. "So it was there in that small upstairs apartment of the girl's student home, that you enjoyed your first simple home together."

Don asked, "Since you've moved around so many years since then, Alma, where would you say home really was for you?"

"That's easy, Don. Home for me is wherever Orvil is."

"That was true for me too," Orvil added. "Home for me was wherever Alma made it so. She changed my life. And she became the subject not only of my day-to-day existence, but also of several of my writings in the years that followed. One of the longest poems I ever wrote -- 47 stanzas in all -- is all about Alma. It told her entire life story in verse form. Here's a copy of it. You can read it when you have more time."

It happened "some few years ago"
Way down in Tennessee,
The cutest little girl was born,
As sweet as babes can be.

All her kindred and their friends
Were captured by her charm.
Mary Alma, this was her name.

Was born on a small farm.

Later came brothers Jim and Bill,
All three formed "The Happy Three,"
As in the woods and flower-strewn fields
They romped with childhood glee.

Tragedy struck the happy home,
When death knocked at the door.
God called their father home to rest,
He left for heaven's shore.

The family moved to a children's home,
In Nashville, Tennessee,
Where Masons' widows and orphans
Might live together free.

There, Alma lived for many years.
When she was through grade school,
She studied commerce, got a job,
It seemed she'd "made it cool."

But then, the mother too, was called
To her reward and rest;
And Alma, with her brothers, faced
By far their hardest test.

For she was barely seventeen,
Her brothers younger still,
But they all worked and studied with
A good determined will.

Now Alma cooked, and washed, and ironed,
From dawn throughout the day.
At night she studied in high school,
No time for rest, or play.

When through college she'd worked her way
As a secretary,

She felt God's call, and soon began
Life in a seminary.

There too, she worked to pay her way,
There she knew need and hardship.
Her faith and courage bore her on,
She knew God's love and lordship.

While there she heard of a missionary
From Mexico he came.
So little he impressed her that
She soon forgot his name.

When at last, she got her degree,
"Master in Education,"
She served the Baptist Sunday School Board
In Christian publication.

One day in Texas Alma went,
To a Baptist Convention,
Good publications to present,
Was her vowed intention.

The Missionary from Mexico
Happened to come around.
When he looked into Alma's eyes
His heart began to pound.

A lonely widower was he,
In the Bible he had read:
"It's best that man not live alone,"
The Word of God had said.

With Alma he talked a good while,
And Cupid winked his eye,
He knew that Orvil would get that girl,
Or make a real hard try.

They said "goodbye" but very soon

107

A mail courtship soon grew.
The mailmen in two nations soon
Their welcomed whistle blew.

Because of war-time censorship
The letters all were read,
So many words were blotted out,
Who knows what each one said?

But Orvil got the message through,
Alma did not say "No."
Soon, off she went to take a look
At his Mexico.

The train was packed with soldiers,
No empty seat was found,
But on her luggage down she sat,
For she was "wedding bound."

They changed her to another car,
Her baggage stayed behind.
She searched, and searched, but all in vain,
Her things she could not find.

Her wardrobe, and her wedding dress,
Alas, had gone away.
What could she do? Then, through her tears
Alma began to pray.

God heard her urgent, tearful plea,
And proved his love and grace,
When at the border she arrived,
Her things were all in place.

She thought that she would get a bed,
Because she did not know
The Pullman crew was on a strike
Down in Old Mexico.

Another night she "sat it out,"
And finally reached the groom,
But she "had had it" until she felt
Just like a worn-out broom.

They went to see the Civil Judge,
Who had the power to marry.
He said, "My friends, I'm sorry, but
You folks will have to tarry.

If you should wait your rightful turn,
Two weeks you'll have to wait;
But if you'll give a nice fat tip,
I'll open up the back gate."

The desperate groom shelled out the cash,
But, had he bribed, or tipped?
The only thing he really knew
Was that he had been "gypped."

Good "Uncle Sam" sent out a man,
Bilingual interpreter,
To tell the bride just what went on,
In words that she could "hear."

The Judge pronounced them man and wife,
Full legal power he carried.
Alma said, "It may be true,
But I do not feel married."

But after, in the Baptist Church,
The sacred vows were read,
A sermon preached and prayers were prayed,
"I'm married now," she said.

A reception in a friend's home,
Then off on the "honeymoon."
Two days to Guadalajara?
Yes, folks, it ended that soon!

Orvil, her husband, was "Papa"
To sixteen big boys, you know.
He'd left little cash with the cook,
So, soon she ran out of "dough."

Before Orvil left to meet his bride
He started a new volcano,
So he would have something real new,
That to his wife he might show.

Shortly before Paricatin,
Began in a field of wheat,
It was spouting ashes and fire,
As lava spread like a sheet.

"Guadalajara Student Home,"
A sign in blue and red,
"Welcome Mother to your home,
Is what her "sons" had said.

Her ten "daughters" lived near by
In the Girl's Student "House,"
They'd come to visit their "brothers,"
And to meet the new "spouse."

Alma's problems, as you might guess
Was bad communication.
She knew no Spanish, English to them
Seemed like a new creation.

Orvil would leave for days on trips,
Alma stayed home with the "kids."
Tears of loneliness must have stained
With red sometimes her eyelids.

A brave soldier, she stood the test,
And soon had at her command
Enough Spanish so she could speak,

And so she could understand.

Soon she helped in the local church,
Also in the Association.
When she was asked to nationally serve,
She felt like "the cows of Carnation."

Ladies "Lib" should give her some cheers,
For, though layman, or preacher,
All with respect and admiration
Accepted her as "Teacher."

A firm tradition had grown up,
One nobody could handle,
That a woman should teach a man
Was the world's worst scandal.

Now, multitudes of both young and old,
Including women and men,
Have been blessed because Alma had
The faith and the guts to win.

Of this multitude there's one man,
Who, far above all the rest,
Give thanks to God because his life
Through Alma, has been SO blessed.

He's bald-headed, has a long nose,
From Oklahoma he came,
Yes, you guessed it; I'm the guy,
And Orvil Reid is my name.

Alma concluded with a smile, "So now you've heard our love story. From then on, I was there. But now that we're through all that part of the story, I think we should stop and decide how we're going to celebrate with some lunch. From here on, why don't we just let

111

Orvil talk, and tell you about some of the other aspects of his life and work with the student homes, print shop, strong man feats, and all the other sombreros he wore as a field man, poet, and innovative-preacher."

"I might even let you read some more of my poems. Some of them are pure cornball, but some of them are..."

"Some of them are going to have to wait. We're going to eat now, Orvil. Give our ears a rest. We know YOU lived all this, but give US a break."

"I'll give you a break -- where's my sledge-hammer?"

CHAPTER 8

THE STUDENT HOMES

Don and Kay had a speaking engagement outside the Ft. Worth area, so they left Orvil their tape recorder, in case he got inspired to share some things over the weekend. When they got back on Monday afternoon, they learned he'd provided a lot of interesting information about a couple of the areas where he wore some of his many sombreros – those were the Student Homes and the Print Shop.

They all arranged to meet the next morning, and they headed back to their motel. Don had hours of work ahead of him, transcribing all that Orvil had recorded over the weekend.

"The Student Homes where Alma and I lived and worked were a large part of our missionary and ministry life in Mexico. Because of the legal restrictions placed on educational institutions outside the United States sponsored by religious groups sent from the United States, the Foreign Mission Board did not think it wise to invest in schools in Mexico. Many people, including me, thought the time had come when we should seriously reconsider, and begin the establishing of schools. The prominent religion of Mexico provided thousands of schools and taught their religion as if the laws did not exist. Since Baptists did not have schools, our best hope for leadership in the future was in the encouragement of our young people to study and to develop in a Christian environment. As Christian schools were not a likely possibility, and the need to help provide that Christian environment was a recognized one, Christian student homes came into existence.

"Remember, when I returned to Mexico following Jewell's death, I assumed a new assignment in the city of Guadalajara. For a while I lived alone in one room of a Mexican pastor's home. In the following weeks, two Mexican students were also invited to live in that home. It was as though God was speaking to me through those students. I became personally aware that the development of Baptist young people presented two serious problems. The first was economic. Many of the Baptist youth were from poorer homes, and for them to have to pay the high price generally asked for room and board in a city like Guadalajara was out of the question. The second problem was a moral one. Many of the Christian young people came to Guadalajara from smaller towns. To be suddenly placed in the environment of a large city with its multiple vices would likely endanger their moral standards. This would especially be true without the warmth of a Christian home to come home to at the close of a busy school day. I knew of young people completely lost to the cause of Christianity because they fell in with the wrong crowd and soon were enslaved by some worldly vice. Only a few of Mexico's state capitals had universities, so most of the young people did not live near centers of higher education.

"It may have been because of the struggles I endured in attaining my own education, but my heart went out to the many young people in Mexico who seemed to have no chance at all to go to school. I remember the day I first met Jose, a thirteen-year old boy who accompanied me to an encampment several hours away. During the drive, I became aware that Jose had a keen mind and seemed hungry to learn, but I also learned that he was not going to school very much during that time in his life. On the return trip, I talked with him, asking him if he wouldn't like to return to school.

"Sure" he replied, "I'd love to, but I have to work nine or ten hours a day in a shoe shop in order to help make a living for my widowed mother and my four brothers and sisters. I've been trying to attend a night school," he added, "but sometimes I arrive late, and sometimes the teachers don't come, so I'm not going any more."

"I arranged to give him the same wages he had been receiving for a full day's work, allowing him to work only three or four hours a day in my office. It was no great sum of money -- three *pesos* a day -- about thirty-five cents -- but it allowed him to go to school. That young man's name was Jose Gonzalez, and that was the beginning of the Student Homes in Mexico. By the time school started that September, two other boys came to live with him and to go to school. All of them stayed in that same room, and ate in the home of Jose's mother. This was all the rather insignificant and humble beginning of the first student home in all of Mexico, a permanent home for Christian students desiring to study in Guadalajara's higher learning centers.

"A student home was just that, a home away from home for Christian students who were studying at a particular city. But each Student Home needed space for housing the students, facilities for bathing as well as for washing clothes, a place to prepare the meals, a place to eat, a place to study, and a place to play and fellowship with one another. We soon rented a building so we could house and minister to more students. We needed a housekeeper and a cook, so I secured the services of a Christian widow who was struggling to educate her five children. This was a real blessing for her and a godsend at the beginning of this new ministry, which grew to

116

become a National Student Home Ministry.

"I'd wondered many times what good could come out of the early hardship years of my own life. We had pinched pennies until Lincoln on the penny yelled. We had scrimped on nickels until the eagle on the nickel objected. We had had to cut back on dollars, until the eagle screamed. But all of that was good preparation for these years, when I had to find ways to make a few dollars on the mission field go a long way. Even the experience of those years when I had to help my mother in the kitchen at home was now helping me to be more aware of what it took to feed my new family. And having to do light housekeeping since an early age, helped greatly, now that I was alone, as I had to do most of it totally for myself again. Of course, when Alma and I married, I had her loving help and support in this ministry, but as you know, that was not to happen for some months to come.

"While I was living in the annex of the church, I was able to save mission money by not eating out, or paying room and board. Also, when I began the student homes in Guadalajara, I was able to be happy eating almost nothing but beans, soup and tortillas, and I found greater joy in sharing almost all I had, including money, with the students who could not pay over fifty cents a day for food and lodging.

"Even without Jewell Starr at my side, or Roderick in my home, I was soon surrounded by the love of many students to whom I seemed to quickly become father, mother, brother, pastor, counselor, and friend. The first three boys in the student home were all named Jose. Of those first three, Jose Cortes and Jose Gonzalez lived there for years. Jose Cortes was just going into high school when he came to the home, but he stayed until he finished law school. He also pastored a small mission about a hundred miles from Guadalajara during those years. When Jose Gonzalez came to the home, he was just beginning the fourth grade. He lived there through all his early school years, and on through high school. He then attended medical school, ranking among the highest in his class. He was a deacon in the First Baptist Church of Guadalajara, superintendent of their Sunday School, a member of their choir, and often preached Sunday afternoons in a mission church. I guess I sort of became the father figure Jose Gonzalez needed at that time in his life. And I grew to feel that Jose Gonzales was something like a son to him. I even wrote one of my poems to him and titled it, from 'A Father To His Son.' "

I am so proud of you, my son,
I fear sometimes I sin.
My heart is thrilled with what you've done,
Each victory that you win.

118

Still, I have not a haughty pride,
It is a heart-felt joy
That simply cannot be denied --
A father for his boy.

I'm proud because I know that you
Are conscious that God's grace
Has led you on in all you do,
Your path God's hand does trace.

I'm proud because you live to serve
Your God and fellow-man;
And thus your life does well deserve
God's mighty, helping hand.

I'm proud, though I may never do
The noble things I dream,
That somehow I may play, through you,
On God's Great Service Team.

"It wasn't long before we rented a house, and Jose Gonzalez's family moved into it. His mother cooked and helped be a mother to all the boys. More requests came in from young people who wanted an opportunity to study. We bought a print shop, so the boys could help earn their way and learn something of a trade.

"I was always looking for new roads to open, so during this time I began taking cars full of young people with me on my trips to Camp Aytec, the only Baptist Camp in the entire country, located a day and half's drive away from Guadalajara. We'd fill the long hours on the road by singing and reciting scripture. Whenever we'd see workers in the fields along the way, or persons waiting or walking on the shoulder of the road, I would blow the horn to attract their attention, and the young people with me would toss hands full of religious tracts out the windows of the car. It was something like a modern day sowing of the seed, for some often fell on unproductive ground, while many fell into the waiting hands of those all along the way. How we enjoyed looking back to see people rushing to the papers, picking them up, and beginning to read them, even before the car got out of their sight.

"When positive reports from the boys' student home reached the ears of the people in the *provincia* of Mexico, requests began to come in from girls begging for an opportunity to study and live in a similar student home for young women. I led the mission to rent another building and thus began the student home for girls. It wasn't long before the Foreign Mission Board adopted the homes for both boys and girls. The first director of the girl's home was Mrs. Claudia Gaspar, the widow of a pastor who had died while in the First Baptist Church in Guadalajara . The biggest problem during those first years was that we had no money on which to run the homes. All my personal salary, and what the poor boys and girls could get together could hardly pay the rent and keep the kitchen supplied with tortillas and beans. We all ate together in a tarpaper shed they built in the patio. We had a long homemade wooden table. There were no knives or forks, so everyone used table- spoons. No one needed knives to eat soup and beans anyway. Many of those who lived there had never even used a spoon before, as many Mexicans in the village use their tortillas as spoons. Only once or twice a week did the Student Home meals include a little meat in their soup. But the students were happy. And they were living in an environment that was cheaper and much better for them than they would have found anyplace else during those years.

"Conditions gradually improved. The first full-time missionary at the girl's home was Mrs. Nova McCormic. Some time later Miss Miriam McCullough became their director. Many improvements in living conditions and in the general well being of the home were made in those early years.

"Students lived in the homes and attended the public or private schools of their choice. Some were still in grade school, but most of them were in the secondary and preparatory schools, which corresponded to stateside high schools and junior colleges. Even in those beginning years, the directors were thankful to have students who were studying in the university in the schools of law, medicine, dentistry, engineering, commerce, and teaching. Several of the students desired to serve the Lord in a full-time Christian ministry, so continued their studies at the seminary. One girl graduated as a medical doctor, two others received degrees in obstetrics and worked as missionaries. Four others graduated as nurses.

"The homes offered special opportunities to the children of pastors and other workers whose meager salaries would otherwise have made it impossible for their children to get an education. As I've already mentioned, the Student Homes also helped young people to receive the secular preparation necessary to later attend the Mexican Baptist Seminary. As a general rule, a student paid what he could and worked to help defray the remainder of the cost. For an investment of less than fifteen dollars a month per student, we had a part in helping prepare those young people to be the future preachers, doctors, lawyers, and teachers of Mexico. The mission work many of them did while in the home was worth whatever it cost to keep them there. What a joy and satisfaction it was to see that most of the young people in the homes were faithful workers in the churches, the majority of them serving as teachers or officers. Many of the boys preached in the growing missions that would soon become the growing churches of that growing city of Guadalajara.

"Everyone involved with the Student Homes looked forward to the day when there would be dozens of professional men and women going out from there each year. We knew that these would in turn win others of their business and professional circles to Christ. One of the problems grew out of the fact that people from a lower cultural, social, and economic level had started some of the early Mexican churches. But we saw a wonderful improvement in that as the years passed. Each year, there were more and more Baptist young people studying in the universities of Mexico. Still one of the saddest things we had to do in relation to this work was to deny many worthy young people the opportunity to prepare themselves for life and Christian service, because they could not pay their way and there was a limit to the number we were able to help.

"One of the special blessing happened in the summer of 1943. Roderick returned to live with Alma and me in Mexico. He had almost forgotten his Spanish during his four years in the States, but it soon came back to him. He and his new mother fell in love with each other at once. It seemed like the full-fledged fulfillment of God's promise as he had been to Job centuries before, for God had given me a wonderful wife, joy had returned to my home and my life, my son Roderick had returned home, and we had the love of all the young people in the

123

Student Home and the church people all over the city. It was also about this time that the Foreign Mission Board began to give partial support to the Student Homes and helped us buy some needed equipment.

"On October 3 of that same year, 1943, the Student Home gained a new resident, when our daughter, Charlotte Ann was born in the Catholic Hospital in Guadalajara. Even her birth gave us an opportunity to be witnesses to what we believed. The hospital nurse became concerned about this baby of the Protestant parents.

"The nurses asked us, 'When are you going to baptize her?' "

"She will be baptized when she was old enough to understand and accept Christ as her personal Savior, and only then, when she asks to be baptized."

"What? Are you going to let her grow up like an animal?"

"In the few days we were there, we had opportunity to speak not only to that nurse, but to proclaim a silent, and at times not so silent witness to the faith in which we built so much of our life.

"Anita grew up to be a beautiful young lady, and learned both Spanish and English at the same time, but spoke Spanish better than English. She also grew up enjoying the benefit of dual citizenship in both the

United States and Mexico.

"Roderick was converted at eight and was baptized at nine years of age. He was a good student, and took an active part in school and church activities. He always loved football, basketball, baseball and track. The years flew by, and it didn't seem that many years had passed before it was time for him to attend high school. We had promised his aunt back in Oklahoma that he might return there in order to attend high school, so we followed through with that promise. Following high school, he attended Tulsa University, where after his sophomore year, he married his high school sweetheart, Mary Lou Fields. They later attended Baylor University together.

"Student Homes were not only significant in the lives of the students who came there to live from other cities in Mexico. In another way, they became home for Roderick and Charlotte Anne as well."

CHAPTER 9

THE PRINTER

"As with the initiation of many other ministries, the Student Home Print Shop also grew out of necessity. When I learned that the National Baptist Convention of Mexico owned no publishing facilities, my thinking-wheels began to roll. It was about the same time in 1943, when the Student Homes were getting going, that we established a print shop in the Student Home in Guadalajara. I had heard of a small print shop that had gone bankrupt, so I used a part of my own small personal savings and bought it. It had two small job presses, and I thought they could just send their work to an outside linotype for their work, and not have to buy movable type, but before long, a boycott started against those who did any printing for the Baptists. The students knew nothing about printing. I knew little more, but I taught the students the little I knew, and we soon grew into a reasonably successful working print shop with two job presses and one large mechanical press. As impossible as it seems, this small shop printed millions of inspirational tracts a year, plus a few books. I wrote many of these tracts and books especially for Mexico. As important as the print shop was to the production of these things, it was equally important as a work project of those who lived in the student home. As you know, many of the students who lived there could not have continued in school if they had not had any work opportunities to help pay their expenses. The print shop gave them employment during that time, as well as giving them valuable training that some of them continued to use years after they left the student home.

"The Baptists also needed their own print shop because of the difficulty of finding a shop that would print their literature. Mrs. Claudia L. Gaspar of Guadalajara was editor of the national WMU paper. In those days, the editor was also the person responsible for all the business of getting the paper printed. Mrs. Gaspar would often spend days looking for a place that would print it for her, only to find that the local priests would threaten to boycott that particular print-shop if it continued doing her work. Under those pressures, the printer would not be able to follow through with his commitment to do the work.

"One printer told her, 'I am extremely sympathetic with the work you people do. However, the priest has five thousand papers a week printed in my shop, and you have only one thousand a month. He tells me that if I continue working with you, he will take his paper to another shop. He also says that his friends will stop giving me their business. That means that he threatens me with a general boycott. I am not a fanatic, but I do have to live, so I cannot print your paper anymore.' And he didn't!

"During the first seven years the print shop functioned, we published many pieces of literature which supported the national anti-alcohol campaign. Other tracts and booklets were based on such themes as stewardship and evangelism. Others shed light on particular doctrinal subjects. The Student Home print shop also printed hymnals for the Mexico Baptist Convention, and thousands of books for Christian writers of various evangelical denominations.

"In 1952, the National Convention magazine was printed right there in our small Student Home Print Shop. This was in addition to the six million pages of gospel and anti-alcohol tracts, the sixty thousand anti-alcohol booklets, ten thousand books on personal evangelism for a national evangelistic crusade, and about sixty thousand booklets on the errors of Catholicism for a Congregationalist doctor. We also did a little commercial printing, which helped with expenses. As always, all the income from the Print Shop went to help pay the expenses of the students who lived and worked there.

"An entire volume could be written about the

way the publishing ministry played an important part in the lives of individuals in Mexico. Most times we had no idea of the impact our tracts and booklets had on the lives of people who received and read them. But when we did receive a letter or a personal visit for someone sharing how a tract or booklet had changed his life, it was often a dramatic one.

"A man wrote from Saltillo, recounting how when he returned home from his work one Sunday afternoon, he found the tract LA FUENTE DE SALVACION (The Source of Salvation), that someone had thrown through his window. It was like a miracle from heaven. He told us that the little paper had made him think of his need of salvation. He assured us that with all his heart he was repenting of his sins and accepting Christ as his Savior, as the invitation on the tract had invited him to do. The man later bought a mail order Bible from us.

"About a year later, an unknown man and a women knocked at the door of the Student Home, and the man said, 'Perhaps you won't remember me, but about a year ago, I wrote you, telling how I was saved through the reading of one of your tracts. This is my wife. I am so thankful that she too, is now a Christian and now we are both members of the Baptist church. We were passing through Guadalajara on the train, and had a two-hour wait here, so we walked out here to thank you personally for the little tract you published. Had it not been for that, we perhaps would never have been saved.' That tract was a message on salvation by grace, translated from one written by Dr. J. D. Grey of New Orleans. It had cost about one-tenth of a penny to publish; yet it had meant the salvation of an entire house.

"After a great earthquake in Colima, I wrote letters of encouragement to the victims. Many had lost loved ones, and most of them had lost their homes. My letters were sent to those victims in envelopes, which also contained a Gospel of Luke and some other evangelistic material. A young man I had known from the University of Mexico, now serving as the pastor of the church in Colima, helped me distribute about two thousand of the envelopes.

"Some years later, I received a letter from a man who had received one of the envelopes of tracts. The man had made a profession of faith and was now sending money for a Bible. Within a few months, I had a speaking engagement in the Baptist Church in Colima, so went by the home of the man who had written me, to invite him to the service. No one was at home, so I left a note, inviting the man to the church service that night. When the invitation was given at the close of the service, the first person to make a public profession of faith was that man. He shared part of his testimony with the group that night."

"When the Bible came, I began to read it every day. My wife, being somewhat fanatical in her own religion, became angry with me for reading it. My parents, as well as hers, also became angry with me, and encouraged my wife to leave me if I didn't give up my interest in evangelical religion. One day, my wife threatened to leave me unless I burned my Bible. I admitted my love for her, but I told her that if she went away and later returned, she would find the Bible still there, for I felt it was important to our lives. As of tonight, she has been gone about three weeks."

"The man was sad, but determined to be faithful to his Lord. We prayed with him, giving thanks for his public profession of faith, and praying that the man's wife would return home. I then continued my trip back down the coast, returning to Guadalajara.

"About two months later, I was speaking in Colima again, but there was no time to visit the man's home before the service. During the service, I was thrilled to see this man enter with a woman by his side. When the invitation was given that night, that woman was the first to come forward accepting Christ as her Lord and Savior. The man came with her, and told me, 'Brother Reid, this is my wife. She came back about three weeks ago. Now I am so happy because we have a Christian home.' All of this was initiated by a gospel of Luke and a tract, printed on the student home printing press in Guadalajara.

"I also wrote and translated many plays in Spanish, which were then printed, presented, and distributed by and through the Students and their Print Shop. One of them, EL COJO TOMAS ENCUENTRA UN GRAN TESORO (Crippled Tom Finds a Great Treasure), had it's beginning many years before, when I read a true story about a little crippled boy named Tom, who was confined to his bed in an attic room. A distant relative whom Tom called his aunt, gave him a meager amount of milk and break that enabled him to barely live. A friend gave him a Bible, and he was converted while reading it alone in his attic bedroom. Tom became convinced that he should find a way to witness of Christ, to win the lost and help the saved to win others. The method he decided on was to write Bible verses and sentence prayers and drop them out the window by his bed, so they would fall on the sidewalk of the street below. His aunt, grudgingly brought him a pencil and a little paper, but he prayed for more paper, to increase his mission project, even if it meant he would have less milk and bread to eat.

"One day a business man was passing by on the

sidewalk under Tom's window and saw one of Tom's notes floating down. He read the note, and became so curious about its writer, that after much inquiry, found Tom in that isolated upstairs attic-room, barely alive. He was deeply impressed by what the cripple was doing, and became convicted of his own indifferent, wasted life as a nominal Christian. He arranged for a nurse to come weekly to see about Tom, and provided him with money for all his needs.

"Later, Tom's physical state worsened, and he died quite suddenly. Before his death, he told his aunt to give his Bible, his only possession, to his benefactor, the businessman friend. As Tom had studied his Bible he had underscored verses and written notes in the margins to make the plan of salvation very plain. He had also helped point out the ways to fruitful service.

"When his friend received the Bible after Tom's death, he gave it to his college student son, who had never been interested in spiritual things. The boy was so impressed by the story about Tom, as told him by his father, that he began reading the Bible with great interest, along with the notes the cripple had written. The college student not only was saved, but he went to Africa as a missionary of a Mission Board, and gave his life trying to win those of that continent to life eternal.

"We presented that play many times in the

States. Because of that play and its message, we saw many lives rededicated to special service. Several people even responded to Foreign Missions following our presentations, so it seemed natural that I would translate it into Spanish, and present and publish it in Mexico. Over 200,000 copies were printed in several editions, and several hundred people made professions of faith at the close of the various presentations of the play. No greater compliment could ever have been given me than for someone to later write that because of Orvil Reid, the Writer and Printer, Mexico was being filled with 'crippled Toms'.

"Now remember, most of our printing was done with old out-dated equipment. Eventually the equipment increased to include a cylinder press, but for lack of anyone to supervise its activities the shop was closed in 1955 and the presses were to be moved to Torreon, where the Mexico Mission was dedicating a new bookstore building in December of that year. Space was provided in that building for a print shop, and it was hoped that the Convention's printing needs could be met in this way. Unfortunately, the cylinder press was accidentally broken in the move, and never provided a satisfactory means of printing the Convention's materials.

"I'm so grateful that God allowed the Student

Home Print Shop to overcome almost insurmountable difficulties and became another arm of our multiple ministries in Mexico."

CHAPTER 10

THE STRONG MAN

"Orvil, while we were away last weekend, I mentioned in our presentation why I was here and what I was doing. When people learned I had the intention of compiling a book about you, one of the first things many people said was, 'You mean, Orvil Reid, the Strong Man?' It seems you made quite an impression on a lot of people with your strongman feats. Tell me about them."

"Well, Don, when was the last time you saw a man lying flat on his back in the middle of a street near a downtown park, with a couple of boards placed over him so the wheels of the truck that was about to pass slowly over his body wouldn't dig into his chest?

And what about watching that same man as he allowed two groups of young men to enact a tug-of-war with a rope which he had wrapped around his neck, while he sang the Happy Birthday song in Spanish? Those were just two of the athletic demonstrations I offered in connection with what I called my anti-vice lectures. For most people, these things became more popularly known as feats of strength."

"But why did you do them? What got you started doing things like that?"

"Those lectures and the feats-of-strength demonstrations were in part the end result of a commitment I made to the Lord many years ago, while I was still a student at Oklahoma Baptist University. As you know, I had always been in the athletic program. At OBU, I was pretty good on the track team. During one of my final student years, Tommy Ryan, a former world's light heavyweight boxing champion visited the campus and gave an athletic demonstration that greatly impressed me. Even though Tommy was eighty-five years old at that time, he still demonstrated his strength by lifting a one hundred pound weight with each hand. To display his agility, he punched an exercise bag with the speed of a young boxer. Finally, to prove his nerve control, he gave a daring demonstration. He showed the students a large sword and proved its sharpness by easily slicing a potato in half. Then a brave student volunteer allowed another potato to be placed on the back of his neck. Tommy stepped forward and with one swift blow of the sword, cut the potato in half, allowing the blade to touch the volunteer's neck, yet stopping it before it broke the skin.

"As Tommy stepped back amidst the applause and cheers of the other students, he said, 'Well, I can see that I now have your undivided attention. Since you are such a captive audience, allow me to tell you something about all this. Many of my friends, boxers and other athletes feel it is necessary to prove themselves to be 'he-men' by drinking and by displaying a generally rough kind of lifestyle. I want you to realize I'm living proof of the other side of that kind of image. I have tried to keep myself free from alcohol and other vices. Otherwise it would have been impossible for me to display the strength, the agility, and the control that you have witnessed here today. But let me be sure you understand that I take no credit for this. It has only been through the Power of God, and my willingness to submit my body, my life, and my all to Him, that this has been possible. Young men and young women, I challenge you to do the same! Oh, by the way, most of my contemporaries are dead now, many of them dying at an early age, due to their dissipated living, and their UN-willingness to surrender themselves to God.'

"All of this spoke generally to the students about their dedication to good and proper use of their bodies. It spoke directly to me. I was so inspired by his plea that I took his challenge, and I determined to dedicate myself to clean living from that day forward. I also wanted to proclaim this to others, however I could, wherever I went. As the Lord led me to minister in Mexico, and I saw young people who were not taking care of their bodies, I was again reminded of that inspired talk I had heard years before. Some of the things I saw in Mexico were not pretty to see. One of my most dramatic poems clearly describes some of those awful conditions, while appealing to my readers for a greater sense of "Compassion and Love."

The stray dogs come and lick his loathsome sores,
He moves a feeble hand, the fly-cloud soars,

The blood and pus are oozing through his pores.

His face and body bear the marks of sin,
A helpless slave is he of beer and gin.
How could a human come to such an end!

Alone, to wallow in the filth and mud,
A twisted mind, a body stained with blood,
The dregs of evil drown him as a flood.

O God, can this loathsome creature be one
Created in your image? For whom Your Son
Died, that even such as he might be won?

Shall we, like the priest and the proud Levi
Gather our skirts, and with disdain pass by,
And leave him in his dirt and sin to die?

My sinful soul revolts against such sight.
But you, oh Christ, did die to give the light
To every soul, no matter what its plight.

And you love this foul creature, Lord Divine,
As you, in mercy, love this soul of mine.
Make our two hearts one, let your love entwine.

Oh let me kneel to wash the filth away,
The foul sores cleanse, and kneeling humble say:
"But for your grace, this man were I today!"

"The sights of drunken men and women lying in the streets or in nearby fields during their pilgrimages made me sad, but it also increased my desire to do something about it. I wanted to do more than hold a mere weeklong evangelistic meeting. My heart ached to begin a campaign against the effects caused by the evils of drink that would help them for a lifetime.

"The opportunity to do so came in Guadalajara, where I organized a national anti-alcohol campaign. As boldly as I could, I tried to let people know about my desires. The governor of the state was openly enthusiastic in his support and congratulations, and he encouraged me to talk about this work every place I could. With the help of students and other volunteers, we began to write, publish, and distribute thousands of tracts, offering free counsel to anyone who was a victim. Such a flood of letters came pouring in that even with the volunteer help, it was not possible to answer them all, or respond to all their needs.

"I prayerfully decided to write a more extensive book, which I titled, *Como Quitarse El Vicio Del Alcohol (How To Get Rid Of The Alcohol Habit)*. In it, I tried to present what I could not present to each person individually -- the need for regeneration and a personal salvation. I wanted to present this need in such a way that even the most fanatical religious believer or the rankest materialist would not be offended. In those early days of self-publishing, it was almost unbelievable to us when over a hundred thousand copies of that book were printed and sold. A smaller booklet of information was edited from the larger book, and was distributed in four different editions in years to come. Federal and state school officials even recommended its sale in the public schools of the city. It was thrilling to receive letters from many of those who had found release from the capture and bond-slavery of alcohol. It was especially gratifying to hear from the ones who had found Christ and eternal salvation. In an unprecedented move, the Southern Pacific Railroad in Mexico gave me and the campaign a couple of travel passes, in order that someone could ride the rails, carrying the campaign along their line. Two students did just that during their summer vacations. At the same time those students took advantage of the opportunity to preach the gospel at every whistle-stop.

"Not only was the anti-alcohol campaign helpful to those who were already trapped by drinking, it also helped others not to fall into the habit. It had always been difficult for a missionary to find an open door into the public schools of Mexico. It was sometimes even considered against the law to hold an open-air, assembly-type meeting. And too, neither teachers nor students seemed very interested in our lectures. I had never forgotten how Tommy Ryan used athletics in the promotion of his campaign for clean living, so I decided to use the same approach in my fight against alcohol. Suddenly I was invited into more schools and meetings in order to give my athletic demonstrations in connection with my anti-vice lectures. I lived and worked with Paul's advice to 'become all things to all people that I might win some.' I couldn't preach as a part of the school-demonstrations, but during my athletic demonstrations and lectures, I often repeated such phrases as 'my strength comes from the Lord' and I would tell my listeners 'how the Lord could help them to live a healthy and sane life too, if they would only trust Him to do so.' I'm not sure all the people who knew me well thought I lived a sane life anyway. Many thought the crazy things I did were just that--crazy! But those folks probably didn't remember Paul's 'all things to all people' idea. I was called a fool many times for giving that program. No one ever called me a fool for playing football and basketball in high school, yet I was injured more in four years of those games, than I was in over forty years giving those programs. But my lectures and athletic demonstrations thrilled my heart and honored my God. They saved souls and led thousands to a happy, healthy, fruitful life. My strong-man feats helped many live forever with the Lord."

"Orvil, I've been to Mexico," Don said. "There are people everywhere, but how in the world did you get them to stop long enough to listen to you? Did you publicize what you were going to do? Did you plaster the walls with posters like the bullfights do, announcing that at a certain time in a certain city, a man would willingly be run over by a truck?"

"Not exactly. On any given day when I didn't have other pressing schedules, I'd fill my old carryall station wagon with a load of young men from the Student Home, and we'd head out to one of the pueblos on the outskirts of Guadalajara. Somehow the word always preceded us that we were coming to put on our show of strength and people would be waiting when we arrived. Others would gather around with just the slightest bit of promotion, encouragement, and invitation. Most folks had never seen anyone attempt any of the things I was about to do.

"When we had a crowd, I would begin to talk about some of the vices of life, like cigarette smoking and drinking, and what that kind of lifestyle would eventually do to them. I'd tell them I was going to show them the benefit of leaving those things out of their lives. I'd invite several of the younger boys in the crowd to join me in front of the crowd. I'd extend my arms, and ask the boys to hang on to them, like they would from a tree limb. Then I'd effortlessly lift them off the ground -- some hanging from one arm, some from the other -- and swing them back and forth, from side to side. The people just laughed at first, until they realized I was quite serious about what I was doing. I didn't mind their laughter, for even when they laughed, they usually stayed around to see what I was going to do next.

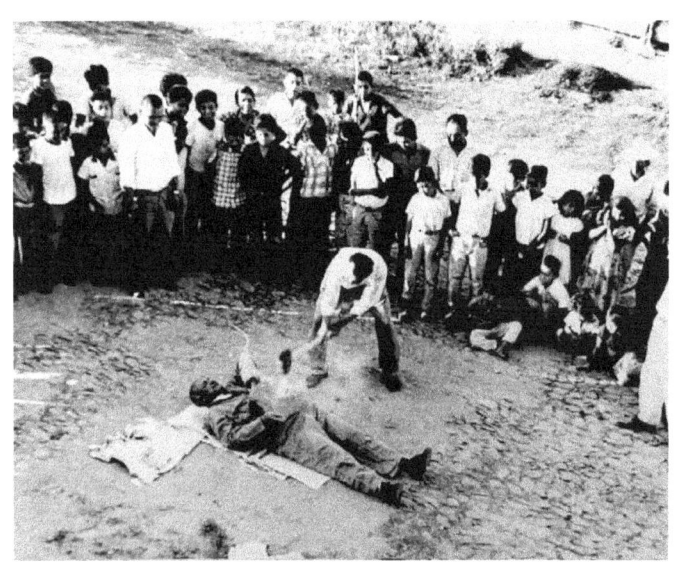

"I'd then challenge the strongest person in the group to take a large sledge-hammer and break a large rock on my chest. There was always the risk that someone would crash the hammer right into my ribcage, or miss the rock completely and crack my head, but I took that risk, and nothing like that ever happened in all those years. Attention-getting feats of strength like these were my calling card. Even if those in the crowd didn't remember me, or my name, I hoped they'd at least remember the God who had called me there, and given me the strength and good health to perform these strongman feats.

"In another trick I'd plant my feet firmly on the ground, then challenge a boy or a group of boys to try to move me or push me over, almost always without their being able to do so. Sometimes I'd sing songs while those things were going on. Think about what I was doing, and then imagine me singing such songs as 'Rock of Ages' or 'I Shall Not Be Moved.' I guess it's not surprising that I became know as Orvil Reid, the Strong-Man!

"Once the crowd was completely involved in it all, I'd speak some words of testimonial about the wholesome physical lifestyle, mixed together with a little preaching, then I'd talk about the spiritual self, and the God who created us, and how that creator-God wanted us to take better care of ourselves. In the course of this part of the presentation, I'd do my famous tug-of-war display. I'd loosely wrap a large towel around my neck, then wrap a long, thickly woven rope around the towel, leaving several yards hanging free on both sides. Then I'd invite groups of men and boys to have a tug-of-war with the rope, while I sang *'Las Mañanitas'*, the Happy Birthday song in Spanish. They tell me I'd often become quite red-faced before it was all over, but I could endure it as long as anyone else could. Furthermore, I'm here to testify to the fact that I always survived to tell about it.

"After a few minutes to regain my breath, I'd

talk some more about God and how He gives each person the good sense to take care of himself. I'd talk about Jesus who gave His life for us, and how Jesus was waiting for some of them to give their lives to Him. I always explained how one could accept Christ into their lives. Probably because of the confidence I'd established through the other things, it was a rare occurrence for anyone to walk away during that part of the talk. And surprisingly, no one ever gave me any kind of trouble at all.'

"The last feat of strength was the one people seemed to remember the most. I allowed the carryall to be driven over my chest. I'd lie down on my back, place a couple of boards over my ribcage, then allow someone -- usually one of the students -- to slowly drive the car over the boards. The people would cheer and clap and yell, '*otro, otro*', which was a demand for another display of strength. But by then, I'd almost finished what I'd come to do. The people were by now convinced that what I was telling them about the better physical and spiritual life was indeed the truth.

"Sometimes without a break in the action, we'd immediately involve the curious throng in a Bible Study or a Bible School. I would often involve whoever happened to be in the crowd -- children, youth, or adults. Once, I even invited a local drunk who remained

148

observing the boys and girls, to find a place and join in coloring the Bible Story for that day.

"If we weren't going to have Bible School, the young men from the student home would distribute those tracts, which had been written and printed by them, about the evils of tobacco and alcohol, and the benefits of good physical and spiritual health. Then we'd load the ropes, the boards, and ourselves back into the carry-all, and head back to Guadalajara until another day came along when I would become 'the strong man in another place doing the same things all over again.

"Orders for the anti-alcohol tracts and books came in from most of the Spanish-speaking nations. All the income from the sale of those books went back into the printing of free tracts. That anti-alcohol literature opened the door of the gospel message and made friends for us among all thinking people. It had an evangelistic as well as a moral value. For that, I'm truly thankful."

"But I read in some of the newspaper clippings you loaned me that you continued doing all these things in other places too."

"Yes, but I think we'll talk about that at another time in the story. Why don't we move on to another area of my life and work? What shall it be, Don?

CHAPTER 11

THE INNOVATOR

"Orvil, I've been told you were quite the innovator when it came to preaching and your use of illustrations. Why don't you tell us about some of the things you did that gained such a reputation."

"Well Don, in my earliest days as a missionary, like most everyone else with that responsibility, I was expected to preach at the drop of a Bible. In order to always have a sermon at hand, I had to be innovative in using what appeared to be impromptu. Sometimes I used extended object lessons in the pulpit. A favorite of mine used a stack of bricks to prove its point. Since almost every church or mission was in some phase of building, this was one object lesson that never suffered from a lack of the common objects at hand with which to properly illustrate it. I'd enter the pulpit with a stack of bricks in my hands. During the course of the sermon, I'd toss bricks into the air from one hand to the other, illustrating how a person's life could be tossed around by the world, indecision, insecurity, and instability. To help make my final point, I'd hold one brick high into the air for all to see, then drop it suddenly, causing my listeners to lean forward in their pews, with almost the entire group making an audibly gasp, for they were sure the brick was going to smash onto the floor of the church. Unknown to them, I was always prepared to catch it firmly in the other hand just before it hit the floor, further illustrating how God's invisible presence is always available in their lives, and how firmly they could trust themselves to be caught and held in His Almighty Hand, if only they'd allow it to be so. Not everybody got the point of such sermons, and there were always some who found my pulpit object lessons more entertaining than meaningful, causing them to laugh at their lessons, instead of applying them seriously to their lives.

"In another object lesson I liked using, I'd display a large glass of clean water, while preaching about all its purity and other good qualities. I'd then take a sip or two of it to show it was good, and even offer some of it to one of the listeners, who almost always would take a sip of it too. Then to that glass of clean, sparkling, water, I'd gradually add printer's ink, or some other murky substance, not only completely changing the appearance of it, but also making it undesirable for anyone to drink after that. The point was then easily made about the life God had given each person, and how easily that life could be contaminated and made impure. I always thought that was a powerful and strong finish to a rather simple idea."

Alma had to get her two-cents in on this one. She told us the story of "how Orvil was also willing to dress up in a costume in order to further illustrate and emphasize his sermon on how sin could imprison one in so many ways. Needless to say, some church leaders didn't consider his black-and-white striped prisoner's uniform, complete with ball and chain to be appropriate pulpit attire, so Orvil wasn't able to use this one as much as he wanted."

Alma had us laughing as she told us about another area in which Orvil proved his ability to be innovative. "Orvil loved to sing. And he often included singing as part of his messages. He especially liked to use choruses. When he began his ministry in Mexico, there were only a few choruses available in Spanish; so again, he had to be innovative as he began to freely translate some of the sing-along and recreational songs he had transported from the other side of the border. One that seems to stick in the minds of many, focused on love for the members of one's family. The repetitious nature of the lyrics used verses like, 'I love my Father, I love my Father, I love my Father, and he loves me too.' It was easy to learn and easy to sing and it wasn't really a bad idea, but apparently the song became overly repetitious to the point of being monotonous, when adding other verses that went something like, 'I love my

Mother, I love my Mother,' and 'I love my brother...I love my sister, grandpa, nephew, etc. etc.' Orvil was genuine and sincere in his use of it, but sometimes all one's most genuine, sincere and best laid plans just don't come out as one hopes and prays they will."

The group's laughter almost drowned out the knock at the door. Alma opened it to greet James and Edith Crane. As they came in, James said, "It sounded like you were having a wonderful time. We're sorry to interrupt, but we thought you were only working on this Orvil-project in the mornings now."

"Oh no, we hit a lick here, and a lick there, whenever the story hits us," Don said. "We were talking and laughing about Orvil's innovative approach to church planting and ministry. Maybe you two have something you can add."

"We'll just enjoy the fellowship," Edith answered. "If something comes up that we can add to, we'll just jump right in."

"Go on Orvil," Don continued, "What were you saying about being a pioneer missionary?"

"As a pioneer-missionary, I had to use whatever ideas I had, but some of the things that had worked successfully in the states, didn't always work as well when transplanted to Mexico. I recall that one of the ongoing themes of church growth emphasized in the states, was, 'To multiply as a church, it has to divide.' At that time, Guadalajara's First Baptist Church was reasonably new in the ministry. It didn't seem to bother the early church fathers that there was only one class for all the adults, another for all the youth, while children of all ages met together in another class. The leaders were just pleased that spiritual progress was being demonstrated by an increased attendance in Sunday School. As with many churches, the large open sanctuary did not easily lend itself to divisions, but I had another idea, based on what I remembered about some of the many stateside churches, which had successfully multiplied their attendance by dividing their space.

"One week, I decided to string wires from one side wall of the sanctuary to the other, and from the back to the front of the church. I bought a bolt of material for a good price at the large downtown market, and proceeded to hang my newly purchased material from those wires. When the people arrived at Sunday School the following week, many of them were surprised at the sight that greeted them. Not only was the church sanctuary divided into small curtained-off rooms, but also the material I had been able to buy for such a good price was a bright red and black print, which I really hadn't paid much attention to. Some of the more conservative ones were not only shocked by what I had

154

done, but also by that material, which reminded them of the kinds and colors of curtains they loosely identified with the gypsy-bands that lived on the outskirts of town. It didn't take long for the church leaders to convince me that they would do all in their power to multiply in their outreach, without the division of their sanctuary into small, brightly colored, curtained-off rooms. Before the following week's services, those curtains, the wires, and everything else was taken down and put out of sight forever."

"You'd have thought he would have learned his lesson from that. But he didn't. One day, he said to me, 'Alma, I don't feel good about having so many children's classes in the same room, although the children and their teachers seem quite comfortable with the arrangement.' I tried to talk him out of whatever he was thinking about doing this time, but he went on with his plan anyway."

"Oh, I remember this one, "James said. "We were new missionaries then, and it made quite an impression on us. Most of the buildings in the city had wire-framed rooms on the roof, used for drying clothes, housing the dog, or simply for storing unused furniture and old gas tanks. The First Baptist Church building also had a flat roof, and that is what gave you your new idea, wasn't it Orvil?"

"Yes, I thought perhaps some wire walls on the

roof of the church could help create rooms that would house some of the classes of young boys. What I didn't take into consideration was that the Sunday School hour began at 11 o'clock in the morning, and by the 12-noon dismissal time, the boys would be baking in the noonday sun, without so much as a small piece of shade to cool under. I also didn't remember the large open skylight-type windows that opened directly from the roof down into the sanctuary. Not only did the windows look down at the other classes meeting below, it became something of a game for the boys in those roof-top classes to amuse themselves by doing the same."

Now Edith added her contributions to the story. "It was somewhat distracting to the older ladies class meeting in the sanctuary below, to look up and encounter the stares of a group of nine and ten-year-old boys leaning out into the windows over their heads, looking for all the world as if some of the boys were going to fall right into their laps at any moment."

Alma tried to keep a straight face as she said, "Remember, I tried to tell him, but he just wouldn't listen. So that project was soon rearranged as well. But in Orvil's defense, I say again, I know he was sincere in his efforts to provide additional classroom space for the younger classes."

"It may not have been what anyone would have

called innovative," Orvil added, "but I once had to use my own creativity in converting a difficult situation into one which perhaps touched the lives of those involved in a way no one ever imagined in the planning stages. On a particular New Year's Day, a couple of days Bible-School had been projected for a particular village. My helpers and I had prepared drawings of animals on colored paper, and had them ready for the participants to cut out and color as part of the activities. When we arrived in the village, we found that most of the men were drunk, which was not surprising, considering the fact that it was something of a typical New Year's Day occurrence. We proceeded to sing some songs and present some of our Bible stories and character stories, then pulled out all the drawings for the handwork and invited the children in the group to come forward and cut them out and color them. Many of the children were all so timid they would not come forward out of the edge of the crowd. The drunken men were not at all timid and asked me if they could take part in the handwork project. I said of course, so soon there were more than two-dozen, half-drunk men down on their knees, like little children, cutting out and coloring pictures of lambs and other animals. Afterwards, the men stayed right where they were, absorbing the brief message with great interest. Before leaving, they even promised they'd return for the next day of activities. The next day however, almost no one arrived. No one ran out to meet the group as it began to set up for the activities. The group encountered a cold and hostile atmosphere. In going from house to house, extending personal invitations to the people to attend the classes, we learned that after we left the previous day, the local religious leaders had told the people that we were bad people, and it would be wrong for them to have anything to do with us. That may have stopped that particular Bible School venture, but it didn't stop me from continuing to try to do innovative things in my work and ministry as often as I possibly could."

"Remember," Alma said, "I didn't speak Spanish with I first went to Mexico, so I had a good excuse for making mistakes. But Orvil had studied Spanish, and in the University yet. Orvil may not tell you about some of the innovation changes and creative usages of Spanish words and phrases, but I will."

"Oh I'll own up to some of them, because someone was always correcting me, after I had said the wrong thing," Orvil added. "But some of these innovative uses of Spanish are of such a nature that probably no one should admit to them."

"We've all made mistakes with the language," James admitted. "Orvil's just seemed to be funnier than

158

most everyone else's.   I remember that one of the missions Orvil worked in met in a small adobe building, with a tin roof, and very small windows. It was almost unbearable in the heat of the tropics.   They were discussing what they could do to keep the heat from getting them down. Orvil had been in some arbors made with bamboo poles for walls and palm leaves for the top, so he made a suggestion. In his best Spanish, he thought he said, "What the church needs is a good arbor." The Spanish word for 'arbor' is '*enramada*', but he had confused his words and used the word '*ramera*' which carried the meaning of 'wicked, sinful woman.' On that occasion, the smiles of those in attendance helped to give away his error, although it was difficult and somewhat embarrassing for some of them to try to explain to him exactly what he had just said to them. And what he had meant to say."

"And once Alma and I were eating in a restaurant owned by some wonderful Christians on our missionary church field. We were served a large dish of fried fish.   As it was placed on the table, Alma exclaimed loudly, 'I surely do like the fish.' At least that's what she thought she said in such a loud voice. But in trying to say, '*Me gusta mucho el pescado*' she had accidentally used the word '*pecado*' which meant 'sin' instead of the word '*pescado*' meaning 'fish,' so in essence what she had just proclaimed in a voice loud enough for everyone in the place to hear was, 'I surely do like to sin.' The Christian owners of the restaurant just smiled, for they apparently knew what she had meant to say, even if Señora Reid had made such an awful sounding announcement.

"I remember when Jewell and I were living in Mexico City and studying in the University Summer School program. Another couple was also attending the summer program. During that summer they lived in a furnished apartment. Their Mexican maid was very efficient in all the work, including the cooking of very good meals for them. On one occasion, they were sharing one of her good meals with some Mexican visitors, when the man of the house wanted to compliment the maid's good cooking. When she brought in a tasty dish, he meant to say, 'Lola is truly a great cook', and to do so he should have used the words, *'Una gran cocinera,'* but he used the wrong phrase and said she was *'una gran cochina'* which implied she was something like a big pig. No offense was intended, and none was taken, but it was another example of how carefully one has to be when beginning to use new words and phrases in a new language.

"Kay, you can probably appreciate this one, being a Sunday School teacher and all. Once a certain missionary was telling a congregation the story of The Good Shepherd. As there were many children present she tried to tell the story in a vivid way for their sake. She told them about how the Good Shepherd had a hundred sheep, and how one of them got lost, and how he left the ninety and nine and went to look for the lost sheep. She described how he heard it going 'Baa, baa,' so he found the sheep, and put it on his shoulder and took it home where he put it back in the pen with the ninety and nine other sheep. The missionary lady noticed many of the people smiling during her telling of the story. Some were on the verge of laughing right out loud. After the service, she asked one of her national friends what terrible mistake she had made. He wanted to spare her the truth, but finally told her how in their language the word for 'sheep' was '*oveja*.' The word she had used throughout the story was the word '*vieja*' meaning 'an old woman'. With the use of that word, she had actually told the story of a man who had a hundred old women in a pen. One got lost, so he left ninety-nine of them there, to look for the one that was lost. Finally he heard the lost old woman crying, 'Baa, baa,' so he found her, and put her on his shoulder and took her home where he put her back in the pen with the ninety and nine other old women. Only their wonderful Latin courtesy had even allowed her to finish the story. But she did

161

learn one good thing that day – the difference between the Spanish word for 'sheep" and the one for 'old woman.' " The four people in the Reid's living room laughed over that one until they cried.

Finally, James was able to speak again. "OK, here's another one on Orvil. At one of his first Associational meetings, the pastors had some project in mind that they wanted to promote, but they felt the need of enlisting the backing of the women of the associational WMU. The story went like this."

"It should not be a problem for us to get the cooperation of the women. Our wives belong to us. We can simply order our wives to do what they should do, and they will lead the other women to follow," one man said. Orvil had not had too much experience with 'ordering women' and did not know the depth of many a Latin man's idea that it is the husband's rightful place to command and the wife's rightful duty to obey. In his poor Spanish, Orvil responded, wanting to say, 'The idea is good, but sometimes wives are a little hard to order around.' He just made one slight mistake. The Spanish verb for 'to order' is '*ordenar*' which is pronounced almost exactly like the Spanish word '*ordenyar*' which means 'to milk.' No one cracked a smile, but after the meeting, a fellow missionary told him of his rather serious mistake in the use of his newly adopted

162

language."

Orvil added, "After I retired from Mission service almost forty years later, I returned to Mexico for a working visit, and visited that same association field. The young preacher who introduced me that night, had known me since he was a boy, and said many things about me that made me feel quite proud. Among other things he said, 'Brother Reid had the determination that would not allow mistakes in the language to stop him from being a good missionary.' That was true. I always felt that in order to learn a new language, one had to use it, and not be afraid of making the mistakes. I said to just laugh at them and keep going. I tried to encouraged others to thank God for their mistakes, for that at least meant they were trying."

Orvil Reid was an innovator in his use of Spanish, in preaching, teaching, using music, and assisting churches to have more classroom space. As with most of us, sometimes his innovations turned out for the good, at other times, it didn't. But that never stopped him from trying to be the innovator he needed to be in order to minister in so many ways.

Before they left that day, Edith said, "Why don't you all plan to have lunch at our house tomorrow, or the day after, and we can reminisce together some more."

"We're on Don's schedule," Orvil said.

"Whatever he says, goes."

"I'm glad to know that," Don answered. "That sounds good, Edith. We'll give you a call to finalize which day we're going to do it. Thanks for helping so much today."

"Come on Edith," James said, "we need to be getting home."

After they left, Orvil gave Don and Kay copies of many of his poems, saying, "You may not be able to use these, but if you can, please use whatever you want to."

"Thanks, Orvil. You've been great to find and loan me your writings and poems. Speaking of that, Alma, you might bring those folders you have there, when we go to the Cranes. We might need to look for a poem or a newsletter." Kay hugged Alma and Don shook Orvil's hand, as he said to him, "Orvil, you've been a great subject for a book. I'm glad I found you."

Alma wrapped arms around Orvil, as she said, "I am too, Don. I am too."

CHAPTER 12

THE HUMOROUS POET

It seems Orvil was always writing. Tracts. Stories. Illustrations. Booklets. And poems. Some of his poems were quite serious. Some weren't. He wrote poems for special occasions, like the missionary appointment of someone close to him. He wrote poems on the occasion of a birth of a child or a death in the family. He wrote poems of encouragement to fellow missionaries. He wrote hymn texts, to be sung to already familiar melodies. He wrote about special emphases in the church's life. He wrote poems to his wife and to his children. And he wrote some poems things just for the fun of it.

Although many of his poems and writings are interspersed into other chapters about his life in this book, the following all come from a little book he wrote in Guadalajara and printed in the Student Home print shop. The booklet was titled, "A Book of Corny Verse." In the introduction he wrote, "This book costs 25 cents each. All income above costs will go to help students in Mexico." In additional cover remarks, he confessed that, "many of these thoughts are not original. Most of them are jokes I have heard or read through the years. I have converted them into verse form, and have no idea of their origin." They are included here exactly as they were originally written. "A Real Success" sets the tone for all of the writings that followed it.

My parents tried their level best
To prevent my being a poet.
Few parents ever had such success:
When you read this, you will well know it.

"The Laugh's on Me," was a proclamation of a truth Orvil lived and believed.

As we laugh, perhaps we'll learn
That humor's greatest wealth
Comes to him who does not spurn
To laugh at his own self.

"Mediocrity" is almost too true to be considered "corny."

I am not broke, but bent,
I'm neither bum, nor gent,
I am not dumb, nor wise,
I'm not the "worst," nor "prize,"
I'm neither short, nor long,
I am not weak, nor strong,
I am not young, nor old,
Not timid, yet not bold,
I strove to be a wit,
But got halfway and quit.
You've guessed it, yes, that's me,
I'm mediocrity.

"Modesty" is all about Orvil and his native state.

Though I believe in modesty,
In it I'm firmly rooted,

But he that tooteth not his horn,
The same shall not be tooted.

So modestly I'll tell my tale,
It may be news to you
That the great oil-wealth of my home state
Is due to my I.Q.

I really thought that my I.Q.
Would be up so high
That they'd have to look for it
Way up in the sky.

But they had to dig so deep
Just to find my rate
They found the first oil-gusher well
In my home state!

Do you think you can guess where I was born?

I was born in nineteen and eight,
Just one year earlier, on the same spot
I would not have been born in any state,
(The name of the state means "Home of Red People.")

"I Was A Peeping Tom," sounds sensational, but it really isn't.

I saw her as she lay asleep,
So lovely and so quiet,
Her graceful limbs were all exposed,
For it was hot that night.

Her curls, like ringlets of pure gold
Were over her pillow spread,
Her skin was fair and soft to touch,
Her lips were tempting red.

Beside her, doll and bottle lay,

167

And still she wore here bib,
I longed to fold my baby daughter in my arms,
But left her there in her crib.

In these selections from "To Us Tiny Tots," he addresses a problem many folks struggle with throughout their lives – the problem of beingoverweight.

Doc said, "You'd better watch that stomach, man!"
Few people mind their docs, I guess, like me,
For I am doing everything I can
To get it out in front so I can see.

I used to play some golf, but had to quit,
For, since the day my manly chest did fall,
When I get close enough to make the hit,
My front won't let me see the pesky ball.

Although the people laugh and make wise-cracks,
Humps serve as reserve, so I let mine grow!
The camels carry their humps upon their backs,
I carry mine in front, as you may know.

Some people tell me that I ought to diet,
They say my big stomach is a horror,
And they are right, I guess, so I'll try it,
I'll eat WELL today and diet tomorrow!

In these selections from "Tenderly Dedicated to All of Us Members of The Great Order of The Shining Bright Dome," he humorously talks about another problem many men experience, including Orvil himself –baldness.

Ma Nature made lots of heads,
Some good, some bad, some fair,
But some turned out so blooming cute,

She had to leave them bare.

Some have a lot inside their heads,
But outside they are bare,
Some heads are empty all inside,
But outside they have hair,
And some of us who go about
Are bare inside and out.

Beware of how you talk about
Us folks who have no hair,
For some who laughed at one baldhead
Were eaten by a bear!

Some people think that I had to be bald,
But that's not the way it happened at all,
When I was born the head angel said,
"We're fresh out of hair, except some that's red."
I said, "Not for me, though it will be tough,
Just let me stay bald, but please, no red stuff."

You know, it isn't bad at all
To have a head completely bald.
If you go out, or stay at home,
You never have to brush or comb.
If you have hair, don't strut or crow,
A few more years may make it go.
If you have none, cheer up and smile,
For baldness always stays in style.

Let's give the baldies a break for the doubt,
Although their peeled heads may be hard like bricks,
For some day our curly locks may come out --
Let's say it's because hair and brains don't mix!

Then, there was a brief writing from "Playing the Game" -- of love.

"Would you sign with me for life?"
Said the Dodger fielder, Simond,
"Sure, I'd like to play, I will be your wife,
If you have a nice, big diamond."

Some of the writings in this collection of corny verse could only be "Miscellaneous."

"What is the difference" was asked of me,
"Between an elephant and a flea?"
Elephants quite often do have fleas,
Don't tell me fleas have elephants, please!

Some of the first students with whom he worked, later became "Doctors," and he loved to give some of them the needle in his humorous verses.

"Doc, this bill's an abuse, it's high as the sky,
That it's too much just can't be denied!"
"No, it's not too high, and here's the reason why
Because I left my fine gold watch inside."

"You should never let your problems
go to sleep with you,"
A family doctor to a wife once said.
Little did he dream just what his words
would make her do --
That night she kicked her husband out of bed.

"Your coughing is better today,
"Well Doc, that should be right.
At least that's what I too would say,
I've practiced it all the night."

"Why can't you take me with you on your trip?"
"Doctor's orders dear, you see
I'm not to take anything -- that's the script,

That doesn't agree with me."

This little verse might not have come from "Sparks of Genius," but the sons described surely thought they were.

> *"My son is the dumbest in all the world,"*
> *One father disgustingly cried.*
> *"Your son is a wizard beside my own,"*
> *His friend with assurance replied.*
>
> *The first gave a dollar to his bright son,*
> *"Take this and buy me a Cadillac."*
> *The lad took the bill" "Thanks dad, for the mon,*
> *Now don't go away, I'll drive it right back."*
>
> *His good friend said to his super-brain son,*
> *"Go to my office and see if I'm in,"*
> *The obedient boy set out on a run,*
> *With a sort of questioning grin.*
>
> *The two lads met, and were both up to par,*
> *"My dad sure goofed! Can you guess why?*
> *He sent me to town to get a new car,*
> *And didn't even say what color to buy."*
>
> *The other sage said, "My dad can top that.*
> *He sent me to the office just to see*
> *If he was in. He's crazy as a bat,*
> *Why, he could have phoned and not have sent me!"*

Here are a couple of four-liners titled "Farmettes."

> *"I can do everything that's done on a farm."*
> *Said a boastful city wag,*
> *Then Farmer Brown said, "Well, while we're waiting,*
> *Would you kindly just lay me an egg?"*
>
> *"I will show you now how to milk the cow."*

171

What the new hand said made the farmer laugh.
"Since I'm just beginning now to learn how,
Don't you think I'd better start with the calf?"

Orvil also had a couple of things to say about "Preachers."

"You're welcome Pastor, to our Liar's Club,
You might win the prize, would you like to try?"
"Why I never told a lie in my life."
"You win!" they all cried, "that's the biggest lie!"

"I'm sorry I preached so long,
My watch needs an overhaul."
His listeners chanted this song,
"There's a calendar on the back wall!"

For a man to be able to laugh at himself so openly, and to lovingly poke fun at the preachers, the bald-headed folks, the over-weights, the redheads, writers, doctors, golfers, ball-players, husbands, wives, farmers, smart people, and those who weren't so smart, plus making some important observations along the way, and doing so with such a sense of humor, revealed a completely different and wonderful side of Orvil Reid -- that of the humorous poet.

CHAPTER 13

THE MISSIONARY

As Kay and Don were talking that night, she said, "Another hat many people remember Orvil wearing was one simply called The Missionary. In the midst of all his craziness, there really WAS good getting done. When I was a nurse working in the Mexican-American Hospital in Guadalajara, I was aware that Orvil did more missionary work by accident than all the rest of us did with all our planning. I recall James Crane once described Orvil's Mission Philosophy as 'having fifteen irons in the fire all at one time, and even though some would go cold, enough would get done with the others to accomplish much.'

"As you recall, in those early years, Orvil was almost entirely alone in his missionary task. Having no other examples to follow, he did what he could to teach and to preach. He WAS the example! Even if some things he did were not well understood, or even if some things were misunderstood, he was at least doing all he knew how to do. Perhaps that's much more than many people are attempting to do at the present time, on or off the mission field.

"Orvil was at home teaching, preaching, exhibiting his strength, printing, traveling, and writing,

173

but Orvil was never 'at home doing nothing!' Think about what you already know about him. At one time he had the Print Shop where he was writing and producing tracts and music, as well as supervising the work at the two Student Homes, plus his on-going anti-alcohol campaign. He also served as the subsidy administrator (an early term for Associational Missionary) for churches in the states of Sonora, Sinaloa, Jalisco, Colima, Guanajuato, and the State of Mexico, as well as author and teacher of his book *'Encaminando al Nuevo Creyente*,' a book about all the things a new Christian needed in his life in order to strengthen his new Christian walk.

"Orvil would often get very involved in the personal lives of the young people at the student home, as well as the lives of the pastors with whom he worked. He once learned that a pastor who lived in one of the villages outside of Guadalajara was living an immoral lifestyle, often visiting the wife of a fisherman when the fisherman was away from home for days at a time. It was also rumored that this same pastor was forcing his attentions on another young lady who lived in that nearby town as well. Orvil knew he needed to somehow confront the situation, but he really didn't know exactly what to do. As always, he came up with an original and creative way to deal with the problem. This was one

174

time when one of the hats he wore really WAS a sombrero.

"On a certain day, he went to that nearby town. As most field men needed to do from time to time, he visited the churches with whom he worked. He learned that the pastor in question had made plans on that very day to make another of his visits to the young woman. According to Orvil's information, the young woman had unsuccessfully tried to ward off his advances, but he didn't seem to want to take 'no' for an answer. That day, things happened just a little differently than the pastor expected.

"He knocked at the door, with his usual distinctive knock. The young lady opened the door just far enough to see who it was, and as usual, began to try to close it. He was much stronger than she was, and began pushing on the door from the outside, saying, 'Don't be like that, Señorita. You know you can't keep me out. Why do we always have to go through this same thing every time I come here?'

"She tried to close the door from the inside. Her voice was strained as she replied, 'No, I do not want you here. I do not want to see you again. Please, please go away.'

"There is no reason to protest, my Sweet Paloma. Just let me in and I will prove to you that what you feel about me is not the truth.

"About that time, a tall Mexican peasant man appeared beside him there on the street. He wore a long dirty serape that reached almost down to his dusty leather sandals, and his face was almost completely covered by a floppy-brimmed sombrero. He spoke in short sentences, with a low, matter-or-fact tone in his voice. '*Que pasa aqui?* What's going on?'

"The woman upon hearing his voice, opened the door, and rushed outside, and began to pour out her part of the story, ending by saying, 'I have told him to stay away from me. Tonight he has come again, and I do not want to see him. He is trying to force his way into my house.'

"The tall peasant stranger asked, '*Es la verdad*? Does she tell the truth?' This time he used a voice that sounded even more angry and gruff than before.

"The pastor gave the peasant-man a slight push with his hand, as he said, 'What I do is none of your business. Go away. This has nothing to do with you.'

"At that moment, the peasant-man threw his serape aside, and pushed his hat back from his face, revealing that he wasn't a Mexican peasant-man after all, but Orvil Reed, that pastor's own missionary friend, who revealed himself dressed as the tall Mexican peasant man. 'I am sorry, Brother, that it had to come to this. I

176

heard rumors about you, but I did not want to believe them. I had to see what was happening with my own eyes, so I disguised myself and waited here at the corner until you arrived. Now I know that what I heard were not rumors, but the truth. And I am truly sorry.'

"It may have been something of a dangerous thing to do, but it was also a courageous thing to do, in order to prevent the same thing from happening over and over again. That was Orvil Reed, the Missionary.

"And then there was Pablo," Kay continued. "Pablo was a man who owned a small grove of oil coconut trees, and the annual harvest brought in about a thousand pesos in those days. He almost always owed most of what he made, but he had been converted, and always saved out his tithe and gave it to the church. Once when the Latin American Mission Secretary, Dr. Everett Gill, Jr. was in Mexico, he heard about Pablo, and wanted to visit him. Orvil gladly obliged. They arrived at the little village where he lived. His house was a simple palm-leaf hut with a dirt floor. Inside, they found Pablo's elderly widowed mother, and his only brother, a paralyzed man who could not walk. And there stood Pablo, balancing as always on his crutches. He had to walk on crutches, because he had had to have one leg amputated just above the knee many years before. He had inquired before about the cost of an artificial limb, knowing that if he could do without his crutches, he could do more for his family and for his church, but found that the cheapest artificial leg they could find was too expensive for him, and they felt they could not buy it. On that day, Dr. Gill asked Pablo if he had never felt the temptation to buy himself an artificial leg instead of giving his tithe. Orvil recalls how impressed Dr. Gill was with Pablo's answer. It was the same thing he had been saying all these years. 'Yes' he replied, 'I did think about that, but I figure it is better for me to go hobbling through life on crutches than for my church to have to hobble along without my tithe.' It wasn't long after that, that a doctor in the states learned about this great need, and arranged for Pablo to receive an artificial leg, completely free of charge. By that time, Pablo didn't need it anymore. The Lord had already called him home, yet the story of his faithfulness in giving has inspired many in the years since."

As a missionary, Orvil was always doing something. At times, he was starting several new projects at the same time, leaving the "work in progress" in the hands of a student pastor or a layman, while he went on to the beginning of the next new project. He was always motivated and pushed forward in all of this by the pressing realization that there truly was a great harvest out there, with many people yet waiting to be won to the Lord, while there were so few workers. One of the messages he proclaimed to missionaries and nationals alike, in word and deed, was "Our All for Christ and The World's Great Need."

God, give us eyes to see the great need
Of a sin-cursed world, a slave to hate,
A world of suffering souls that plead
For life and love, before it's too late.

God, give us hearts to feel the deep pain
Of a world that gropes in dark despair.
Help us, O Lord, to remove the stain
Of stolen tithes, and neglected prayer.

God, give us hands that delight to serve
Instead of those with the selfish grasp.
God, give us feet that will never swerve
Till earth's ends have the Message at last.

Give us eyes, and hearts, and hands, and feet
That count everything but thee, as loss.
Oh help us Lord, till the last heartbeat,
Carry the truth of Christ and the cross.

With our eyes, hands, feet, voice, mind, and soul,
We would be faithful till life's last breath.
Living and teaching the Story of Old.
We would be faithful Lord, unto death.

Many people write books, others paint pictures; some compose music, while some create poems for their own self-satisfaction and/or occasional and incidental gain. Whether it was through the use of object lessons, sermons, songs, choruses, or simply rearranging interiors of churches, or dressing up like a peasant in order to

179

straighten out a problem or doing strong-man feats in order to attract a crowd, Orvil did all he did for the advancement of the Kingdom's Work in Mexico. He did it all so that people could come to a saving knowledge of the Lord Jesus Christ. His challenge of Mexico to missions was one that meant sacrifice and loving patience, requiring Christian people to ask themselves the question, "What Does It Mean to You?"

What does it mean to you, if souls
Sink down in the depths of sin and shame?
What does it mean if they miss their goal
And never hear of Jesus' name?

What will it mean if one you love
Finds himself in a devil's hell,
Not having known of God's great love,
When you have known but failed to tell?

What will it mean if some shall say,
When all are judged by God on high,
'You failed to tell, I missed my way
And since you failed, my soul must die.'?

What does it mean that day by day
Millions are born to eternal night?
You are their hope, you know the way.
You have the keys to life and light.

What will it mean when you've reached the end
To see souls lost because of you?
You failed your God, they died in sin.
God says their blood remains on you!

The message must be proclaimed even in the face of occasional unpleasantness and minor persecution.

180

Orvil often wondered how it would feel to face a mob of howling fanatics. "Would it be possible to love and not hate?" he thought. "When the test came with its jeers and flying stones, a feeling of deep love and pity filled my heart. I could not help but have a feeling of respect and even admiration for the people whose religious zeal made them willing to fight for their faith. They were like Saul of Tarsus who thought he was serving God when he was persecuting the Christians. After receiving three blows of small stones in the head, and leaving Las Flores, Jalisco, with a shower of stones hitting the car, I think the meaning of our Lord's words on the cross were more easily understood, 'Father, forgive them, for they know not what they do.' Many of our most faithful Christian workers once were fanatics who hated evangelicals and were ready to do them harm."

Orvil and his family often knew exactly how it felt to be the direct or indirect object of scorn and hatred. There was a wave of persecution in Guadalajara in the middle 40's. The persecution took different forms. Knife-wielding people attacked some of the men from the student home as they were on their way home from church. Revival services at a local church were interrupted by about three dozen students who attended, but demonstrated their opposition by shouting so loudly that the speaker could not present the message. Orvil attempted to get help from the sub-police chief, who refused to try to establish order, because it was a Protestant church.

Orvil and Alma's own home was stoned ten times in one month. One particular night, gas bombs were thrown in through the windows. They were so poisonous that they couldn't use the room for three days. On another occasion, three men stoned their house, and a rock broke the wire screen and the windowpane, scattering glass on the bed of their little daughter, Anita. This time, Orvil took matters into his own hands. He waited around the block thinking that if they returned, he'd be ready for them. They did come back, throwing rocks at his house again. He caught one of them and held him until the police could be called and carted the fellow to jail.

Other children often tormented the Reid's eight-year-old son Roderick, as he walked home from school. Once they dragged him three blocks in order to force him to go to their own church. Orvil always felt that these were tests on the part of certain church officials, hoping he would give them an excuse to start a mob, or to give them an opportunity to have him removed from their country. Some of their leaders had taught them that the evangelicals were as bad as the communists, and that they did not believe in God, and that they hated their

Virgin Mary, and that evangelical missions was just a ruse of the United States to attempt to conquer Mexico.

Orvil maintained his Christian spirit, and later wrote, "Mexico on the whole is not this way. The minority makes a lot of noise, but the gospel must win out in Mexico. The people are heart-hungry for something that will satisfy their deeper spiritual longings. We cannot expect a people who have suffered spiritual bondage for hundreds of years to find freedom for the masses suddenly. It will take patience and love, but in the long run, truth must win."

Orvil Reid the Missionary giant, truly had a giant helping of patience and love! When he found "Forgiveness" to be hard, he often had to remember the truth expressed in his own poem on the subject.

'How oft shall I pardon my brother?'
Once Peter the Lord did ask.
Just seven, no doubt, would be legal,
Once more would make hard the task.

'Not seven, seventy times seven.
An infinite number? True!
Have you even counted, dear Peter,
The times I've forgiven you?'

I too, so often, like Peter,
Have found forgiving so hard,
I need at times to remember
How oft I've offended the Lord.

God, give me such love and kindness
That others I may not offend.

Help me when other offend me
To forgive them, yes, times without end.

CHAPTER 14

THE SERIOUS POET

As you have read in a previous chapter, Orvil had all the capabilities of writing humorous verse, and of taking somewhat commonplace subjects and setting them in humorous rhyme. Perhaps one of his least-known abilities was that of using verse as a means of proclaiming inspirational messages as well. Some of his poems were quite serious. He wrote poems for special occasions, like the Missionary Appointment of someone close to him. He wrote poems on the occasion of a birth or a death in a family. He wrote poems of encouragement to fellow missionaries. He wrote hymn texts, to be sung to already familiar melodies. He wrote special poems for special emphases in the church's life. He wrote to his wife and to his children. He compiled many of these poems into another small collection in 1970. This was one of the last books, which was published in Guadalajara, again with "all income from the sale of the book, above actual publishing costs, going to help students in Mexico." *Anchors for Life's Storms* was a book that highlighted many of the personal storms, which had touched the life of Orvil Reid as he had gone through his dozens of years of missionary service. I don't think he ever doubted that people didn't take him seriously, but I sincerely believe he knew many people did not relate him to this kind of writing. Therefore, in the introduction, he attempted to explain to those readers who were more aware of his humorous or corny verses that "many of these verses were born out of deep emotional experiences, or of firm moral and philosophical convictions. Many friends have told us that some of these verses printed in pamphlets have helped them. The publishing of this book is but the earnest effort to extend the scope of service. We will be happy if some fellow-traveler over life's road finds something in these verses to inspire, comfort, or edify." All of the following selections are edited from that small paperback book, and for the most part, speak for themselves in regard to their inspiration and basis for being written and for the subject matter they express. The title page also included Orvil's own introduction.

Two hundred twenty-one messages in verse
in forty-two topical divisions --
A practical philosophy for daily living.
Enter doors to beauty, peace, joy, hope, comfort and
security.
View new horizons of the meaning of God, man, life
and death.

May my verse like a flower,
A rich healing fragrance release,
That will fill you with comfort and power,
And bring you deep joy and sweet peace.

186

Though it may be that it remain unseen, alone,
Still I'll sow, for sowing brings a joy all its own.

There is value in each of his writings. Hopefully, one of these chosen from his collection "Anchors for Life's Storms," will somehow be exactly the one you need to read at this particular time in your life. An excerpt from another newsletter will help introduce the first of these serious writings.

"YOUR MEXICAN VISITOR: Feb. 29, 1960 - Some of you have already heard of the death of our fifteen-year-old daughter Charlotte Ann (Anita), Feb. 12, in Houston, Texas. It has been so hard to realize that it has really happened. Of course, we cannot understand it, but we can still trust; and we know that Romans 8:28 is true.

"We have been trying to think of what we have to be thankful for, instead of our losses, even in this sorrow. In the first place, we are thankful that God gave us Anita, even though for a brief fifteen years. She was so full of life and joy. She loved people and loved the Lord and his work. She loved Mexico with all her heart, and longed to help the people here.

"Many have asked about her sickness. In December she had a severe attack of headache and vomiting. Dr. Lamar Cole, our medical missionary, suggested that we take her to the hospital. After a couple of days, she seemed all right and wanted to come home. The doctors were making all kinds of analyses, and wanted to keep her under observation a few days longer. They found that there seemed to be some pressure on the optic nerve near the brain, as revealed by the eye-gram. They suspected a brain tumor, but none of the tests indicated it.

"After she had been in our hospital in Guadalajara for a week, she returned home. When the condition did not clear up after a month, the specialists here advised us to take here to some good medical center in the United States.

"We took her to Baptist Memorial Hospital, Houston, Texas, to a noted brain specialist. She still felt fine, but the doctors knew that something serious was wrong. Again many tests and X-rays were made, but no tumor showed.

"The doctor said that they would have to put gas into her brain through her spine to see if the X-ray would show up the tumor. As always, she was in a cheerful mood as she left for the test; and she had the doctors and nurses laughing at her jokes as they prepared the anesthetic. We all thought that she was going just for a test, and in case an operation was necessary, it would come later.

"After about an hour, the doctor came to us very worried. He said that the abnormal pressure of the fluid in her spine would not allow the gas to get to the brain, and that he would have to perforate the skull and put the gas in directly. Other X-rays were then made and a tumor was revealed on the left side of her head.

"The doctors were going to operate at once, but suddenly Anita stopped breathing. After some time she breathed again, and they began the operation. Her breathing then stopped once more, but they had to continue the operation while giving her oxygen and artificial respiration.

"The anesthetic was given at 10:30 in the morning, and she never regained consciousness. At 1:30 a.m. Friday, February 12, her soul left its earthly abode.

"The doctor thought that he had removed all of the tumor, but the autopsy revealed that there was still another large part down deeper in the brain. The doctor said that even if she had lived after the operation, she might have been paralyzed or disabled in some other way.

"He told us that even before the autopsy revealed the tumor that was left. So we thank God that he took our daughter while she knew almost nothing but happiness in this world."

Orvil realized how much he needed that spiritual anchor during the personal storm following her death. The poem "If" was written onthe morning before her funeral service. Before the poem in his collection, he writes:

"Charlotte Ann (Anita) Reid was born October 3, 1944, in Guadalajara, Jalisco, Guadalajara: mother, Alma Ervin Reid; father, Orvil W. Reid. At eight years of age she made her public profession of faith in Christ and in June 1959, at Ridgecrest Baptist Assembly, she offered herself for special Christian service. She had surgery and never recovered. Her body awaits the resurrection in Guadalajara, where she was born and reborn. This poem expresses the heart-longing of both father and mother."

If just one soul should come to Thee,
And thou that soul shouldst save,
We'll understand 'twas best that we
Should weep around this grave.

If some should dedicate their all
To serve Thy loving Cause,
With joy we'll drink this cup of gall,
And praise thy wondrous laws.

If we can better understand
The depth of human woe,
And better serve our fellowman
Thank God our child did go!

We only ask, O Lord, that thou
Wilt ever near us be:
And then, we know that we somehow

Can bear this Calvary.

Readers of "Your Mexican Visitor" received this stunning report in the July 18, 1967 edition of the newsletter:

"Mary Lou, our daughter-in-law was speaking over the telephone from Gold Beach, Oregon: 'It is about Rod,' she said. 'Rod is with the Lord.' It can't be true, we told ourselves. Surely, there is some mistake; our son Rod, the athlete, was always so full of life.

"He and a high school student were out in a motorboat in the ocean. When they failed to return, the sheriff's office was notified, and a search began. Next morning, the pilot of one of the search planes sighted the over-turned boar: later in the day, the two bodies were found about half a mile from the boat.

"Someone wrote: 'First, your only daughter, and now your only son.' We don't know why, that is in the hands of the Lord. We can only say: 'The Lord gave, and the Lord hath taken away; blessed be the name of the Lord.' "

For most people, losing their only daughter would be enough grief and enough of life's storms for an entire lifetime. Orvil passed through these waters twice, for now his only son was also taken from him by death. In "An Erroneous Announcement" he talks about that event. Again, a page dedicated to the memory of his son precedes the poem.

"Roderick Allen Reid, born in Pryor, Oklahoma, February 7, 1936: mother, Jewell Starr Reid; father, Orvil W. Reid. He was saved by faith in Christ as his personal Savior at the age of eight. He attended Tulsa University, Baylor University, and graduated from

Wayland Baptist College. He served as coach and teacher for six years. On June 19, 1967, he was drowned in the Pacific near Gold Beach, Oregon. He loved to sing, preach, and to work as a personal soul-winner. His favorite solo was 'In Times Like These, I Have a Savior (in times like these, I have an anchor, I'm very sure my anchor holds and grips the Solid Rock).' "

The poem itself was written on the way from Guadalajara Mexico to Jay, Oklahoma, in order to attend his funeral.

It has been announced that our son has died,
That his body is lifeless cannot be denied.
His body was only his house of clay,
And empty has been since he went away.

Our son is not dead, for he cannot die!
Please let me tell you the reason why:
Christ knocked at the door of his heart one day
And asked to come in forever to stay.

He opened his heart and let Jesus in,
Then Christ saved his soul and forgave his sin.
Who has life eternal can never die,
Or God himself would be telling a lie.

Our son has left earth's sorrow and night
For Heaven's joy and eternal light.
On earth, he loved God's praises to sing,
Now he lives with his Heavenly King.

May all who listen, repent and believe,
And with all your heart Christ Jesus receive.
You too, can shout the victor's glad cry:
"I've life eternal, and can never die!"

Perhaps Orvil wrote "Treasure Hold" in a pensive and

191

reflective moment, as he thought back over parts of his earlier life. Or perhaps he wrote this poem in order to help himself work through some part of that intense pain and grief after losing important elements of his family. Whatever his reason, it is a simply beautiful expression of some simple and beautiful treasures he wants to keep forever in his memory.

So thankful I am for her sweet baby smile,
And that we could see when she learned to walk.
For her baby chatter, her very own smile,
And thrills that we felt as she learned to talk.

Thanks for the day when she first went to school,
A scholar at two in her kinder-land.
For the glow in her eyes at her first Yule,
With her toys and trees that she thought so grand.

Thanks for the happy time down at the sea,
Swimming, or hunting for pretty seashells.
For thrills as together we climbed a tree,
While the air echoed all her joyful yells.

Thanks for the wonderful high school days,
For the thirst that she had, new things to know.
Thanks e'en for the state of the boy-friend craze,
That showed just how fast a young girl can grow.

Thanks for the memories in the House of the Lord,
As together we prayed, and read and sang,
Thanks for the day when she chose to go forward
And dedicate all to her Savior and King.

Who lives with sweet memories of daughter, or son
Is rich, though a pauper to some he may be.
Far greater than riches, or fame some have won
Are memories my children have given to me.

June 15, 1960 - We do not question the "why" of the sorrows of life, but we do pray for greater faith to endure the trials. The following lines written by Orvil a few days ago explain what we are trying to say, titled "Faith Shines Through the Shadows."

O Lord, it is so hard this time
To say "Thy will, not ours be done.
Give us, we pray, the power sublime
To pray as did thy Holy Son.
We cannot understand the pain,
The suffering of our heavy cross;
But help us Lord, new heights attain
By all we humans might call loss.
Give us, through suffering, purity,
Through it, obedience may we learn.
No matter what our test, may we
Not doubt thy wisdom and concern.
All things must work somehow for good
To them who love and trust the Lord.
Could we but stand where Jesus stood,
We'd know our lot is not so hard.
And so through tears, with hearts that bleed,
We raise our faces toward the sky:
Our hands reach out that Thou mayst lead,
And to Thy love we leave the why.

In the midst of such trials and griefs and heart-rending memories, Orvil somehow was able to exhibit one of those lives filled with happy and positive characteristics. Some of those characteristics were the very things that rubbed off on everyone he met. People seem to positively identify Orvil with those characteristics. Maybe that's why it was so easy for him to express these thoughts so freely in his writing titled

"Attitudes and Happiness."

Some let one small cloud hide all the blue sky,
They see only thorns and miss the sweet rose.
Some see but problems and give up and cry,
Forgetting their blessing while counting their woes.

Some folks in good health go looking for pains,
Some never see favors, but look for slights.
Some brood over losses, forgetting their gains,
To some there're no days, life's filled with black nights.

Some never see stars, they only see mud,
Never hear music, but only hear noise.
To them, life's still waters are like a dread flood,
They see haughty pride, instead of quiet poise.

Life is so beautiful to those who see
The positive side of things every day.
But sad must the lot of everyone be
Who lives in the negative all life's way.

We all have our share of burdens and cares,
We all could give up in shameful defeat.
But courage and faith can route harmful fears,
And help us life's problems joyfully meet.

Some look for the good instead of the bad,
They major on love, faith, hope, joy and peace.
They try to make others happy and glad,
And their happiness will daily increase.

So what is that intangible something that allows one to be called "a serious poet"? Someone else might qualify by serious attempts to open new channels of thought, while yet another might try a different way of expressing those thoughts.   In Orvil's case, it was perhaps the contrast he evidenced between his enjoyable, light and corny verse, and these more pensive, reflective, and weightier issues, so beautifully expressed in serious ways. Perhaps, it was none of the above, but in his

 own way and in his own serious verse, he has left us something of a legacy of serious thoughts expressed in poetic form, that have gained for him that one additional title, Orvil Reid, the Serious Poet.

CHAPTER 15

THE FIELDMAN

It's shocking to realize that for a time following Jewell's death, Orvil was the only missionary living and working in the entire country of Mexico. From 1940 to 1944, he lived and worked in that same upstairs one-room apartment where they had planned to live before her death. He rearranged the furniture to allow for a table and chairs in the middle of the room. There, he and Elia Gaspar, one of the daughters of the pastor of Guadalajara's First Baptist Church, who worked as Orvil's secretary, spent hours answering the stack of mail that arrived daily in response to the anti-alcohol campaign. Elia remembers that at times there were so many letters that the two of them simply couldn't answer them all.

Only one passing through those days, struggling to just hold on until help could come, could fully appreciate the blessing God gives to those ministering in other countries through Southern Baptists. Orvil was truly grateful for all the support missionaries got. Yet, even in Orvil's day, statistically there was one only missionary trying to proclaim the message for each million people needing to know of Christ; and the missionary's budget was so small that several local churches in the Southern Baptist Convention had a larger monthly income than the entire mission received to support all their field work and institutions in the whole nation of Mexico. Orvil's comment made in 1953 is just as true today as it was then. He said, "We still have to go a long way to be able to do honor to the name Missionary Baptists. His hope was that Baptists would keep praying and giving through the regular Cooperative Program and the especially designated Lottie Moon Christmas Offering, until God brought in a new day for missions, not only in Mexico, but in all the world. His "Prayer for World Missions" written some years later expresses many of those same powerful hopes.

God, give us the spirit of Lottie Moon,
The spirit of love and of sacrifice,
Keep our wavering hearts forever in tune
With Him who, for love, once paid the great price.

Undernourished bodies, now starving for food
Beg for the crumbs that are oft thrown away.
Christ had compassion on the multitude:
Give us that love and compassion, we pray.

Millions are sick, and are not doomed to die,
Our mission offerings so many could save.
Break our hard hearts Lord, until we shall try
Our very best to save these from the grave.

Children and youth to dark ignorance are doomed.
They beg for a chance to study and learn.
Our gifts could set free those minds now *entombed:*

God, make our cold hearts with compassion burn.

Multiplied millions, as yet, have not heard
That on Calvary's cross Christ died for man's soul,
Our offerings and prayers could give them God's Word,
Their souls, sick in sin, could then be made whole.

Christ, our King's business demands we make haste,
The harvest is white, the precious grains fall.
Save us, O Lord, from our greed and waste,
And help us respond to thy urgent call.

The missionaries located in different cities in the U.S.'s nearest Foreign Mission field, make up the Mexico Mission. This group meets annually in order o give reports, make plans, and present budgets, while other committees meet during the year as the need arises. Although they all have their own separate jobs, they are all working with one consuming purpose and goal before them -- Mexico for Christ.

Orvil Reid's field was wherever there were people who could be reached for the Lord. He was well aware that a few denominations had emphasized goodwill or social-center work. In some cases however, the evangelistic motive was lacking to the extent that such services had degenerated into a purely 'social gospel' approach. Perhaps that practice made Baptists often go to the other extreme, to the extent that they lost sight of the opportunity of using social work as an effective means of winning souls to Christ. In those days, Orvil felt Southern Baptists had sadly neglected that practical phase of the work in Mexico, so he decided to remedy that situation.

There were only two day nurseries on the Northern Baptist field and two on the Southern Baptist field, so in 1947, a small house was rented in Guadalajara where a good will center was established. The center offered classes in reading, writing, arithmetic, sewing, drawing, physical culture, English, and piano, along with a few others. Teachers were recruited to work on a strictly volunteer basis even though they taught classes three times a week. Eva Sierra, a graduate of the Torreon Seminary became the director of the center, while at the same time continuing her nursing studies. Activities included ping-pong, story hours, and other recreational and social past-times.

Soon they were able to buy a larger piece of property, which provided more classrooms as well as additional space for a children's playground, and a volleyball and basketball court. It was on this property that they also began a kindergarten and day nursery. In spite of the active propaganda the local religious leaders tried to spread against them, even threatening to excommunicate any who came or allowed their children to come, the center enrolled as many as one hundred and fifty adults, youth and children in its programs. In order to teach that many people, night classes were added to the schedule.

It was soon possible to begin holding worship services there, and the work grew until a church was organized in that very building. That church continues to minister today as the Second Baptist Church of Guadalajara. After the organization of the church, the night classes were suspended, but the day nursery work continued, for it had grown so large that its planning took practically all of the time of the director.

Based on the success of that outreach venture, Orvil began another Bible study in another part of town. Graciela Gaspar remembers how, as a ten year old, she and her mother would walk from what was then downtown Guadalajara, to the location of that Bible study, about an hour's walk from home. There, they'd teach Bible classes for all age groups. For some months, all of these classes took place in a small store at the front of the house owned by a newly converted man. This as how a new work often began. On Sundays, they met there again. Graciela and her mother would leave after First Baptist Church services around 1 PM, prepare and eat lunch with their own family, then walk at least an hour again in the blazing Sunday afternoon sun to meet Orvil there. Sometimes, that ten-year-old taught the youth, while her older sister led the children, and her

Mother taught the adults. They didn't have any prepared materials, so not only did they have to study a lot, they had to create the handwork between Sundays. After some time, Orvil helped buy what was then just a corral for housing animals. A goodwill center and day nursery grew out of those initial contacts. So did that mission. It too grew and needed to be organized into a church. In the first year, they baptized sixteen of those who had come to the center, and there was always a group of people in new Christian classes, awaiting their baptism. Melrose Baptist Church of Houston, Texas and the First Baptist Church of Guadalajara gave spiritual and financial support to this new growing mission, which became Guadalajara's Third Baptist Church, a church, which is actively ministering to people in that part of town even today.

Where just two years before there had been only one Baptist church in that city of almost half a million people, there were now two, and another that should be organized soon. The ministries of the student homes and the goodwill centers contributed greatly to that growth. Their social and cultural service also aroused the interest of many people who never before had any use for the evangelical religion. Those involved in these good works now had many doctors, lawyers, and other professional people who were their friends and stood ready to help them in any way.

On one occasion, Orvil was going to inaugurate a small chapel in one of their missions. Twice, fanatical mobs had attacked the place, and they had to call Federal Troops out to protect the lives of the people. He was more than a little concerned at what might happen when they held the dedication of the chapel there. There were classes all week in the building, some teaching reading, writing, mathematics, shorthand, and typing, so they called the mission a "Centro Social Cultural" or Cultural Social Center. By this time, his old friend Miguel Aleman had become the President of Mexico, so he wrote the president's mother, with whom he had visited on several occasions, and shared the problem with her, suggesting that it would indeed "be an inspiration to the people of the town if she would send a wire to them, congratulating the town upon the inauguration of their new Centro Social Cultural." She sent the wire, and the officials of the town felt obligated to attend the service of inauguration and dedication, in order to read the telegram from the mother of the President of their nation. Apparently, those who had attacked them before were so impressed by all this that they never received any more threats of persecution.

The state inspector of kindergartens helped to inaugurate the day nurseries and expressed her willingness to represent them before the government if that need ever arose. The state inspector of public schools, federal school officials, and even colonels and generals of the Mexican army helped them with their programs. Orvil felt they needed to do more of this kind of work but felt they should always keep in mind that it is not to be an end within itself bur rather a means to a more noble end, the salvation of the souls of men.

Orvil was always appealing for the people at home to pray for more missionaries, as he did in this paragraph from YOUR MEXICAN VISITOR, Nov. 23, 1943:

"Please pray with me that the Lord will send some more missionaries to Mexico. Brother Neal just wrote that he and Mrs. Neal cannot continue the work in the North field because of her health. They have literally worn themselves out in the Lord's work here, and are far past the retirement age. I have written Dr. Maddry to please try to find someone for that field. I cannot do justice to the nine states where I am, for in five of them there is no Mexican missionary to help, and but few pastors.

"Besides the field work, the National Baptist Convention named me as chairman of the committees on evangelism, stewardship, and tract publication and distribution. I am also president of the National Young People's Encampment and director of the Student Home. Would also like to at least halfway be a husband to our newest missionary to Mexico.

"I am praying that several young people will feel impressed to write Dr. Maddry and to offer themselves for work in Mexico after reading of this great need. Please have a special prayer in your church and college groups to that end. Perhaps someone who is out of college and seminary could come at once to help hold the fort until other help can come.

"Pray for us as we pray for the world mission field. Will probably not have time to write again before Christmas so will say "Merry Christmas and a Happy New Year!""

When Orvil was a very small boy, his parents gave him a plot of ground for his very own garden. He was thrilled as he planted a few seeds of many different kinds of vegetables there. His father had explained to him that for every seed planted, there was something of a multiplication of that seed when it came time for the harvest. He says he learned at least two great lessons from that first garden.

The first was patience. Each morning from the first day, he was up at dawn, standing there at the edge of his garden, fully expecting to see the garden full of plants. Slowly he learned that he had to not only sow the seeds, he also had to water, cultivate, and then patiently wait for the harvest.

Once after planting some of the pennies from his piggy-bank in a special row in the garden, he also learned that money does not grow on plants or trees, neither should it be planted in the ground.

As a missionary fieldman, there were many times when he had to remember that he had to wait for the spiritual harvest, after sowing the Seeds of the Gospel. How many times he wanted to see the immediate results of some project. Yet, like his childhood vegetable garden, there was always that time of anticipation, watering, cultivating, and patiently waiting for the harvest, if indeed it even came when he could observe it. He also learned that money invested in the Lord's Work on the mission field brings a wonderful harvest that richly blesses both the giver and him who receives it.

He concluded the December 1965 issue of "Your Mexican Visitor," with his poem, "The King's Business Requires Haste."

It's now or never! What a thought
To make us do our best
To win the souls Christ's blood has bought,
How dare we fail this test!

With each heartbeat, ten people die,
Ten bodies turn to earth,
And twenty babes are heard to cry
As they are given birth.

Awake, ye sentinels! Warn mankind
Of the approaching doom:
For millions march now, lost and blind,
To a dark, Christless tomb.

If we should fail, this countless throng
They face hell's hopeless night:
So let us pray and work and give
To lead them to the Light.

CHAPTER 16

THE RELIGIOUS POET

My singing's bad, I cannot play,
Would that my life might be
A song of love, of hope, of joy,
Of perfect harmony.

I cannot paint, nor can I carve,
But I would do my part
To help some fellow traveler grow
True beauty in his heart.

How vain and empty are mere words
To tell what's in the soul.
Would that my life might be a poem
To tell what's left untold!

Orvil was ahead of his time in his poem about the need for a sense of world brotherhood, or as he called it, "Man's Dilemma is Still: Christ or Chaos."

The world is so full of hatred and greed,
Conflicts in politics, races and creed,
So few think of others; but centered in self,
Most fight to rob others to increase their own wealth.
Few live to serve others, they make life a game
To increase their power, their fortune and fame.
Their hatred and fear, suspicion and pride
Is not something local, but is worldwide.
The nations are banding, those near and afar,
And hearts are all trembling for fear of World War.
The soldiers are training, science works with a will
To learn to perfection the best ways to kill.
The dollars by millions are spent every day
For airplanes and ships, and bombs for the fray.

Though nuclear bombs, and all arms shall increase,
They bring not protection, contentment and peace.
When real understanding and brotherly love
Shall reign in men's hearts, we'll know the Peace Dove.
It seems man's forgotten that God's on His throne,
And that all earth's people and things are his own.
The Lord of all Wisdom, all Love, and all Power
Still longs to help man in his dark, crucial hour.
But till man obeys the great Prince of Peace,
Cruel hate will be King, and wars will not cease.

If those who support missions around the world could read Orvil's poem, "The Christmas Star," and see the on-going reason for continuing to do all that they do, there were be less talk about how it should be done or even whether it should be continued in some instances. And if missionaries and others who serve their Lord in some fulltime way could also re-discover the reason for "The Christmas Star," even their lives and ministries might be dramatically changed.

Heavenly Star that shines above,
Symbol of joy, hope, peace, and love,
Lead us on our pilgrimage here,
In life's dark moments, be thou near.

Lead Mexico, the USA,
And all the world to Christ, we pray.
Lord, help us work, and pray, and give
That all lost men may hear and live.

As Christ on Calvary paid the price,
Help us to make the sacrifice
That we should make, that men may see
Thy love in us and come to thee.

Help us in love to keep our tryst
And give that men may know our Christ.
In all the world may joy-bells ring
As all earth's people praise our King.

Even though it's been said many times before in many similar ways, there is still strength and meaning in Orvil's poem, "My Prayer."

God, help me to be what you want me to be,
Take out all the sin and dross.
From selfishness, greed, and all evil set free,
Lord, humbly I'll take up my cross.

And help me to always be patient and true.
Give vision, O God, from above.
Whatever the task that you'd have me to do,
I'll do with a will born of love.

Lord, help me to suffer the grief and the pain
That tempt me to stray from thy way.
When storm clouds hang low, and cold nights bring
rain,
In faith let me wait for the day.

I'll not be impatient, nor grouchy, dear Lord,
Nor pine for the things I have lost.
But counting the riches I have in your Word,
In love I would carry my cross.

Oh, keep me e'er cheerful and smiling, I pray,
With ne'er a complaint, nor a frown.
If the cross I'm carrying seems heavy today,
I'll change it some day for a crown!

Most people have had spoiled pages in their own book of life, so they should value and appreciate the simplicity of the idea expressed in "The Spoiled Page."

208

I started out that lovely day
With a page so clean and white,
Determined I would keep it so,
That all evil I would fight.

But oft in thought, or word, or deed,
There would come some ugly stain,
And though I tried with all my might,
I would stain my page again.

I grieved, not just because my page
Was so stained with mire and dirt,
My heart was sick to know each blot.
Would my Teacher's great heart hurt.

With tearful eyes at close of day,
With misgivings, shame and fears,
I gave my Teacher the spoiled page,
Then His kind eyes filled with tears.

I stood all bowed with guilt and shame,
How could I have been so mean!
The Master spoke: "I love thee child!
Here's a new page. Keep it clean!"

Surely, no one was better qualified than Orvil, to write "When Testing Times Come."

Whenever I'm tempted to think of self,
Forgetting humanity's need,
Should I think too highly of this world's wealth,
Let thy love constrain me, I plead.

Whenever I'm tempted by loathsome sin,
And hell's deadly darts do assail,
Help me remember that wonderful Friend
Whose love and whose power never fail.

Whenever I'm feeling forsaken and weak,

And seem to be losing the day,
Help me ever thy nail-driven hand to see,
And find strength and courage, I pray.

When I shall come to the end of life's trail,
And death my last strength then shall drain,
I'll rest with my Christ, whose love cannot fail,
For to die in the Lord is gain!

"On Wings Of An Eagle" is based on Isaiah 40:31.

Whenever I'm down in the valley deep,
And everything's cloudy and dark,
A presence I feel makes my heart to leap,
And my soul soars high as a lark.

On wings of an eagle I'm borne on high,
Above all life's muck and its storm,
Then my soul in peace serenely can fly,
Where nothing can threaten or harm.

Then, when I return again to the earth,
My feet firmly placed on the soil,
It seems I've experienced a grand new-birth,
And eagerly face my life's toil.

In "Christ, the Greatest Miracle," he speaks about the miracle of His birth, the miracle of His life, the miracles He performed, the miracle of His death and His resurrection, the miracle of His ascension, and the miracle He performs simply by living through us, and the miracle still to come of His triumphant return.

Christ was a miracle in His birth,
In Him God-incarnate come to earth,
Without earthly father, Virgin-born,
Which unbelievers still laugh to scorn.

210

Christ was a miracle, his sinless life
In earth's putrid valley of sin and strife
Was doubtless contrary to nature's laws.
For all other men are weak and have flaws.

His power over nature, the wind and sea,
O'er sickness and death never could be
If He were only an ordinary man.
A miracle only this bridge could span.

Christ was a miracle in his death,
His enemies blessing with His last breath.
The sun hid its face, and the earth did quake,
When He, on Calvary, died for men's sake.

When Christ conquered death, and rose from the grave,
Mankind from death's sting forever to save,
That it was a miracle none denies,
Unless subtle doubt has blinded his eyes.

A miracle true, Christ Jesus has wrought
Through the basic principles that He taught.
True faith in Christ always lifts to new heights,
While doubt's a curse that belittles and blights.

When Jesus ascended, all were amazed,
As out of their sight He went as they gazed.
The words of the angel made their heart burn,
When he told them that their Lord would return.

So, there's a wonderful miracle still,
When divine prophesy God shall fulfill.
We know not the day, but in God's good hour,
Our Lord will return, in triumphant power.

"Jesus Our All" addresses many of the "common" things attributed to Jesus.

211

Jesus is LIGHT that shines each day,
Giving us warmth and power.
Jesus is JOY that comes to stay,
Cheering each passing hour.

Jesus is LOVE that sweetens life,
Make each hour the best.
Jesus is PEACE in times of strife,
Giving us quiet and rest.

Jesus is HOPE when dark despair
Conquers the weary soul.
Jesus is COMFORT in our care,
STRENGTH and a POWER untold.

Jesus is FRIEND in time of need,
LOVER without design,
LAWYER, who stands our case to plead
At the great Bar Divine.

Jesus is PRIEST, and KING and LORD,
GUIDE to the path He trod,
He is the great ETERNAL WORD,
He is the LIVING GOD.

His singing may have been bad, and he may have been unable to play an instrument, yet through his writings and his poetry, his wish expressed in "A Poem I Would Be" came true, for his life became for many, a song of love and hope and joy, a melody of more perfect harmony. So what if he felt he couldn't paint or carve, he did his part to help many fellow travelers realize true beauty in their hearts. The last verse of that small poem is a typical Orvil Reid understatement:

212

How vain and empty are mere words
To tell what's in the soul.
Would that my life might be a poem
To tell what's left untold!

There is no doubt that along with all the other things Orvil Reid accomplished in his life, he was also an outstandingly dedicated and serious writer of poetry, and his life *did* become a poem which many people will continue to read for years and years to come.

CHAPTER 17

THE ROMANTIC

Don and Kay were nearing the close of their scheduled time in Ft. Worth, so they arranged to have lunch with the Cranes the following day, with some more remembering time to follow.

Edith had prepared a delicious Texas tortilla soup and a hearty guacamole salad, and they finished it off with stateside flan. It was as good as any other good meal they had enjoyed during their years in Mexico.

After a comfortable time for lunch to settle, but not quite enough time for a comfortable siesta, they gathered in the Cranes living room so Don could briefly review the sombreros Orvil had worn, then he guided them into that day's discussion, saying, "Many who knew Orvil only as a Student Worker, a Printer, a Field Evangelist, or a Writer of Humorous, Serious and Religious Verse, would likely not have known him to be romantic in nature, so let me hear it from those of you who knew him best. Was he romantic?"

James was the first to speak. "He wrote many things that revealed that truly underlying nature. One of them was a prose account entitled 'Saint Anthony Is On The Job.' I've kept a copy of it for all these years."

"Do you know Saint Anthony's specialty? If you could go to the great Saint Anthony Church in Mexico City on the day dedicated to this saint, you would see thousands going to visit him. Rows of women as far as you could see for several blocks, from before daylight until late at night, waiting to be able to kneel at his altar. And do you know why? I'll tell you, but don't tell anyone else, or all the girls will start packing for Mexico today.

"You see this is the cupid saint. The married women go to ask him to send them children, or perhaps, to ask him not to send them any more. The single girls go to ask for sweethearts.

"There was a missionary in Mexico who was a widower with sixteen 'children.' There was a young lady working in the Sunday School Board at Nashville, Tennessee, who wanted to be a foreign missionary. There was a Southern Baptist Convention meeting in Texas. The convention, the young lady and the missionary all went to Saint Anthony (or San Antonio, Texas). The missionary was trying to find some new ideas for his work in Mexico. He wandered into the Sunday School Administration Booth. There was the young lady just bubbling over with ideas. She gave the missionary some literature and they chatted awhile. He learned of her dreams to be a missionary. She heard about the needs in Mexico.

"Conventions do not last long, but Saint Anthony works rapidly. He was really on the job. When the missionary returned to Mexico, he wrote to the young lady. She answered and that was the beginning of a wonderful mail-order courtship. The missionary beat the Chamber of Commerce in his description of the wonders of Mexico as a vacationland. The young lady began to dream of snow-capped volcanos, or tropical palms, of beautiful beaches, of student homes, and even of a bald-headed missionary. Just one little last push by Saint Anthony and two Southern Baptists had a Convention in Mexico, when the young lady went there on her vacation. After the vacation, the good Saint had things going his way. It seemed certain that the Sunday School Board was going to lose a good worker to the Foreign Mission Board. Orvil was going to get a wife, and the sixteen students would have a mother."

Then Alma contributed her two-cents worth on the subject. "As we were beginning a new life together, it's little wonder that he wrote this romantic poem 'To My Wife' at that very point in his life. I've committed it to memory."

You are my life's crystal that heaven sent
To fill my days with a rose-colored tint.
You are like beautiful music to me,
Blessing my life with a sweet melody.
You are like rain to the dry, thirsty earth
That changes life's sadness to refreshing mirth.
You are my life's springtime that brings the sweet
flowers
After the winter's cold, dark, dreary hours.
You are my sunshine, life's sweetest perfume,
Without you my life would be like a tomb.

When I am careless, or don't understand,
Just give me a wave with your magic wand
That sparkles with patience, love and sweet smiles,
And, hands clasped together, we'll share life's miles.
When you're marooned on an island, it seems
I'll be your Friday to serve in your dreams.

"Edith, what about you? Surely there's something you can add to all of this."

"Oh yes. This is one of those classics that was told on Orvil for years among the folks in Mexico. Orvil and Alma have always recalled the story just a

216

little differently, but either way, it makes for an interesting account. As you know, he had been a widower several years when he met and married Alma. During these 'widower-years' he had continued his involvement in all the same kinds of works and activities as usual. Some of his time was spent driving to the smaller pueblos outside the larger city of Guadalajara. These were not leisure-trips, even though they were often leisurely made, if Orvil could 'slow himself down enough' to do ANYthing at a leisurely pace! There were always tracts or books to deliver to someone awaiting them, but in order not to make a trip out just for that, he would arrange a personal contact with the local pastor or the layman in charge of the mission or the church in that area on the same day.

"Well, It seems that shortly after Orvil returned to Guadalajara with his new bride, he needed to make one of those trips to a town on the outskirts of Guadalajara. At supper the night before, he surprised Alma by saying, 'Tomorrow I need to go out to one of my churches and pastors. Now I know you haven't had much of an opportunity to get away from the Student Home and Guadalajara since you got here, so why don't you rearrange whatever plans you have made and drive out with me?'

"It didn't take Alma but a moment's thought to

reply, 'Oh Orvil, I'd love to! It will allow me to see part of the countryside surrounding Guadalajara, which I have never seen. Oh yes, I'd love to go! You know how much I enjoyed traveling with my job in the states. It always gave me the opportunity to see new places. Yes, I'd love to go!' The opportunity to see new places was one exciting prospect for the small trip, but another thing she might have been thinking was that since she didn't see her new husband as much as she'd like to, this trip would give them some time alone together driving going out there and back in the car. How romantic it all sounded!

"She neither spoke nor understood much Spanish at that time, so before their arrival in the outlying town the next day, they mutually agreed that rather than accompany Orvil on his rounds, spending time in situations he needed to attend to, and in conversations she would not comprehend, she would just enjoy some time alone in the little flower-lined plaza in the center of town while he went on to do the few other things he needed to do on that particular trip. She could enjoy the sun, the flowers, the children playing near the little fountain, relax, and walk around the neatly trimmed, shady plaza, and he would come back for her after he finished all the things he had to do. She didn't mind, for that would still give them the ride out and the

218

ride back to be together.

"By the middle of the afternoon, Alma had pretty well enjoyed the sun and the flowers and had done about all the things she could do, and seen all the things she could see, and used all the Spanish and the smiles and nods she could get by with there in the little plaza, but she wasn't particularly worried, although Orvil's business did seem to be taking longer than he thought it would. She figured Orvil had just gotten involved in talking to some brother in the Lord, and the minutes had rolled into hours and the time had just gotten away. So, like the obedient new missionary wife she was, she just continued to enjoy sitting there, occasionally changing her position from bench to bench, where she could keep an eye on the street, so when Orvil pulled up, she'd be able to run out to meet him, and they'd share with each other all the wonderful and exciting things they each had done that day.

"What she didn't know was that Orvil had finished his running around long ago, and had gone back to the Student Home without her. After all, he wasn't used to having her with him, and he had absolutely forgotten that she was awaiting him in the park. One of the student home boys asked about her, and for the first time in several hours, he remembered that he had told her to wait for him in the park, some distance back down the road. He knew that by the time he got back there, it would be almost dark, but he took off once again.

"Some hours late, though many hours later than he had planned, he arrived at the designated corner of the plaza, and sure enough, there sat Alma, seemingly patiently waiting for him. As she ran over to get into the car, she seemed to be in a surprisingly pleasant mood. He rather innocently greeted her with 'Did you have a nice time in the plaza, dear?' It wasn't long before he had told her the entire story, and because it was just the way they were, they both had a good laugh over it. The sentiment of a poem Orvil wrote titled 'Forget You?' has a more serious intent than that particular event, but we always wondered if somehow it grew out of a time when he forgot his new bride and left her sitting in a plaza in a small *pueblito* for most of the afternoon.

> *When the birds of the forest forget their nests,*
> *And the mother forgets her child,*
> *When the sun forgets to go down in the west,*
> *And the caged beast forgets the wild,*
> *When the ocean forgets to follow the tide*
> *That tugs at the heart of the sea,*
> *When the lover sincere forgets his bride,*
> *Perhaps then could I forget thee!*
>
> *When the sands of the desert forget the rain*
> *That makes them blossom with flowers,*
> *When the suffering soul shall forget the pain*
> *And minutes forget to form hours,*
> *When this humble heart shall at last become still,*
> *And this body left without breath,*

I'll never forget you, let come as come will,
Forget you? Not even in death!

"Orvil, don't you even want to defend yourself? Or do you think you really are a hopeless romantic?"

"Of course. Let me think which of the many things I need to say. Surely no one I knew, especially not Alma, served as the model for this humorous verse about a newlywed cook.

"Please bring me my coffee honey,"
He said to his new young bride,
"I'll bring it to you soon darling
As soon as it gets fried."

"Kay," Don said, "ever since we married, you've always told me about some advice Orvil and Alma gave newly appointed missionaries. Just for sake of the record, why don't you tell me again?"

"Well, Don, I remember them saying how important it was for couples to take time to be with one another. They would say, 'Now you're going to be busily studying the language, learning about the culture, getting involved in the work, traveling, reading, writing, visiting, leading conferences, teaching, and hosting groups of people in your home. Sometime in all of that you are likely going to feel that in all those scheduled things, with all your meetings and busyness, in the midst of all your multiple ministries, you don't have time for one another. Our advice is to schedule some time for

221

one another right from the start, right along with everything else. If you decide, for instance, that every Tuesday night will be the night when you and your spouse can spend time together, either at home or doing something together at home, and that is marked on your activity calendar near your phone, then when someone asks either of you about something they want you to teach or do or lead or attend on that particular night, you can say with all honesty, 'I'm sorry, but I see we already have a commitment for that night.' Then stick to it! Believe me, spending time together, having time for one another, is one thing you must not neglect.'

And Orvil and Alma practiced what they preached. Whether Orvil was "the romantic" or whether it was Alma, no one is sure. Whichever it was, they faithfully followed through with that scheduled time for one another. On those "date-nights," as they called them, they would go out to eat, just go for a walk in the part, or attend a show or some such routine activity. The thing was to do it "together." Sometimes they'd choose to merely stay home and spend time doing nothing more significant than just talking and sharing with one another.

James Crane was dying to get back into the conversation. "But I remember them telling about one such date night they drove out to a deserted spot 'to park' and enjoy being away from the city, where they could just watch the stars. Sitting there in their car with the windows down and the cool breeze blowing through their hair, holding each other close while they whispered 'sweet nothings' to each other was wonderful. But when time came to head back home, Orvil discovered too late, that where he had pulled off the road, the dirt was soft and the tires were firmly imbedded in some soft dirt, and no matter how much he tried, Orvil couldn't budge the car. It was funny at first, until the realization hit them that someone would have to walk back to town for help. Being a long-distance runner, Orvil convinced Alma that it would be best for her to stay with the car, while he ran back to town for help. He did, and soon, he and some of the Student Home boys were back, and quickly got the car out of the trouble. Orvil and Alma got a lot of good-natured kidding for a long time about their going out to a deserted spot just to neck a little, and having to recruit help to get the car out of the ditch."

"I'm quite certain that Orvil the Romantic was NOT the subject for it, but another of his short poems which I read just this weekend, poked fun at husbands who said they loved their wives with words, but not with actions. This is what he wrote.

"I wish I had a thousand arms, my dear,
I'd use them all your pretty neck to hug."
"I'm not so sure, you'd waste them all I fear,

Cause you're not using them you got, you mug!"

"Orvil and Alma had a genuinely loving relationship," James Crane added. "Most of the time they were quite openly demonstrative with their displays of affection. Sometimes they liked to hold hands during meetings or church services. Once this casual habit almost got Orvil into hot water. During one of the evening services at the annual Mission Meeting one year, they selected their seats, then waited for others to arrive before the worship started. Alma left her chair to talk to another missionary lady just as the first hymn was announced. She and the other lady then just sat down where they were, but as it turned out, the other missionary lady ended up sitting next to Orvil. He, intensely involved, as always, in the goings-on of the service, didn't seem to notice the change of seating-order. At some point, he casually reached over and placed his hand on the knee of the person he assumed was his wife. Not finding her hand at that moment, he quite seriously and affectionately, but innocently, began to squeeze the leg that he encountered there where Alma should have been sitting. Needless to say, the other missionary woman was a bit shocked. She tried to stare at Orvil, but he was totally engrossed in the service. She interpreted his involvement in the service as an unwillingness to even look at her. As he continued to fondle her leg, it brought an even greater mixture of feelings to her mind.

"It was not until some minutes later, when something brought his attention to what he was doing, that he looked into the eyes of the woman on his left, with whom his hand was still making innocent contact with her leg, that he realized it wasn't Alma. Orvil quickly removed his hand. During the singing of the next hymn, the ladies quickly changed places again. Following the service, Orvil had people roaring with laughter, as he recounted the situation to them. Even the other woman found the situation amusing, as have generations of other missionaries since, as this story of Orvil Reed the Romantic has been passed along from one to the other.

The very nature of Orvil's work kept him away from home much of the time. On one such trip to Huixtla, Chiapas, late in his missionary career, on June 3, 1972, he wrote the following romantic ditty to Alma, titled "The Case of the Missing Rib." A note, which accompanied the poem said, "This came out of my heat-cracked brain last night. Now, don't worry, I think I'll be all right if I ever make it to the beach. Folk along the way send *saludos* (greetings) and are praying for you."

I am telling you the truth, Alma, and I don't fib,
I am down in the dumps when I don't have my rib.
You ought to have been with me on this trip down the

coast,
You won't do it really, but you think you will roast.
I'm eating tamales of iguana, but that is just fine!
But I always dream of lizards after I dine.

I waded across the river, then the car got stuck in the
sand,
But "man, I'm having fun in this Promised Land!"
I'm eating lots of bananas and mangos, for they are
cheap,
But I hate the stinging scorpions and other things that
creep.
The flies and mosquitoes keep playing in my hair,
Like a hoard of country people at the county fair.
But all the "brothers and the sisters" no place can beat,
But like a fattening hog, they all make me eat.

My skin has had to stretch so much it's now real tight,
But I keep on eating -- for that's a traveler's right!
But there is something badly wrong and I do not fib,
It's really hard for me to get along without "my missing
rib."

He signed it, "Perspiringly Yours, Love, Orvil W. Reid"

"And I'm not sure for which 'Wedding Anniversary' I wrote the following poem. It could serve for almost any of them, but I think it does an adequate job of presenting me as the romantic the world always thought I was.

Another year we've journeyed, side by side,
Together we'll walk on, whate'er betide.
Not all our pathway has been strewn with flowers,
For we have had some thorny, painful hours.
Not all our skies have been so clear and blue,
Nor all our clouds were of a rosy hue.

226

Black clouds rolled, lightening flashed, and storms
blew fast,
We wondered if the bark we sailed could last.
But through dales, through vales and over hills we trod,
Still, through it all, we see the hand of God.
God, let us meet and love, then made us one,
We know he'll lead us on as we've begun.
Our love and understanding too, will grow
Until we see life's sunset's golden glow.
Together we will sing a song of praise
Because we share together life's sweet days.

They all agreed. They also agreed to go their separate ways for this afternoon, but agreed to get together again the next morning around 9:30.

CHAPTER 18

THE OTHER MISSIONARIES

"Good morning, everyone. James and Edith, I'm glad you're still with us."

"We wouldn't miss this opportunity for anything. Where are we headed with Orvil's story today?"

"I think we're about to draw it to a close. After all, one man can only wear so many sombreros. But there are two areas I'd like to touch on today. One is his relationship with the other missionaries, and the other is Orvil Reid, the Friend."

"Between the two of us and Kay, we should be able to talk rather completely about him in relationship with the other missionaries," James added. "Orvil had a good reputation with other missionaries in most areas, but there was one area in which he shared a bad reputation with many others. That was the area of being a safe driver. Driving in Mexico has always been something of a challenge. One must not only be in good control of what's happening with his own car, but he must also be on the defensive as to what is happening with all those around him. Orvil was a little careless in both those areas. Although in later years, he often boasted that he had never had a serious accident, but that certainly didn't mean he wasn't the near-cause of a few. Most of the people who rode with him were just so grateful that they didn't have to walk, that they were often somewhat hesitant to mention to the good brother how carelessly he drove. At least that was the respectful attitude most of the young people held toward Brother Orvil."

Kay remembered that there were at least a couple of ladies who weren't so young anymore, who had absolutely no qualms or difficulties in telling him exactly how they felt about his driving skills, or the lack of them. "Claudia Gaspar was one of those ladies. As the wife of the pastor of Guadalajara's First Baptist Church, she worked with Orvil both there and in many of the missions of the church. Although she and her children often walked to many of the places where the Bible Studies and missions met, they were able to ride with Brother Orvil from time to time, if schedule and space permitted. He had the same habit many other folks have, of doing a lot of talking while driving along. He also enjoyed pointing out some sights out the side window, while giving a running commentary at the same time, such as, 'Just look at that little burro out there. Why, he's so loaded down he can hardly walk. If that old farmer would only lighten the load just a little, that delicate little animal would be able to make several other trips today. As it is though...and, oh, just look at the color of that field there in the distance with the sun shining on it in that way. It looks just like...' Not only would he talk about those things in the near and far distance, he felt he had to also point them out with a wave of his hand or his arm. His problem was not just that he talked while he drove, or that he gestured while he talked. It was that he would turn his eyes away from the road; even turning around to look at and talk to the person he was talking with. This wasn't too bad if the person was seated beside him in the front seat, but when that person was in the back seat, his eyes were completely off the road. And when that person was Señora Gaspar, she would politely interrupt him by saying, 'Mister Reid, please watch the road more carefully. I assure you that I can hear your words to me here in the back seat, without your needing to turn around and talk to me while driving. As for all the things along the roadside, I can see them quite well myself. Thank you for pointing them out, but I would really enjoy them more if we were not on the verge of having an automobile accident.' And with a smile, as though it really made everything she was saying totally acceptable to him, she would add, 'Thank you Mister Reid.' And Orvil would begin to softly whistle a hymn, hoping the moment of chastisement had passed. It wasn't long however before he'd see something else, and begin to point out everything else again, letting his eyes wander from the highway all over again. And she wasn't hesitant to reprimand him again!

Even Orvil had to learned to laugh about his bad driving habits. But as he told it that day, "Even Alma, my usually sweet and soft-spoken wife, had a way of calling my attention to something I had done or not done, by simply pronouncing my name in her own distinctive and attention-getting way. Anyone who knew her well, knew exactly what she was about to do. Her method was especially effective when she thought I was less interested in looking where I was going than to whom I was talking. She'd first give me a brief, but hard look. If that didn't get my full attention, which it seldom did, she'd enter into phase two, when she'd snap her head back away from me and tilt it to one side or the other, and firmly purse her lips as though she were going to whistle, but instead of whistling, she'd draw in a deep breath which made its own sort of whistling sound as it filled her lungs, then directing all of this pent-up air and energy to the task at hand, she'd pronounce that one word 'Orvil' as only she could. She had her own way of saying the first syllable very low and drawn out, dragging it along into a rising inflection, until she arrived at the last syllable almost screeching out the last sound in such a way that even 'Ooorr-viiillle!!' had to take note of what I was doing."

"Do if for us now, Alma," Don pleaded. "These other folks may have heard it, but I never have."

Alma was glad to get in on this story. She gave Orvil a long, hard look, then snapped her head back, and tilted it to the side, then pursed her lips, drew in that long whistling breath, then let go with a low, drawn-out, rising-inflection pronunciation of that one word, "Ooorr-viiillle!!" It was so effective, that Orvil jumped at first, as though he'd been caught doing something bad again. Then the entire room-full of people enjoyed another good laugh at Orvil's expense.

After Orvil settled down again, he said, "I guess I could have used myself as the subject for one of those this funny little four-liners I included in my *Book of Corny Verse*. Even though I wouldn't admit it at the time, I knew I drove somewhat carelessly."

"Somewhat?" Alma laughed

"Yes, somewhat" he answered. "And even though the humor here is a bit dark, I can still laugh at myself."

> *Two fellows were driving around in their car.*
> *One said, "We're approaching a town.*
> *It must be a fact; I know that we are,*
> *For I'm knocking more people down."*

Kay remembered one rainy afternoon, "when Orvil offered to drive me and my Mother, who was visiting from the States, to a Mexican circus. We could have been going anyplace else, but on that particular day, it was the circus. As always, he was also dropping off somebody else on the other side of town on the way to wherever he was going, so Mother and I went along for the ride. It was a typical white-knuckle, grip-the-back-of-the-seat, does-he-see-that-other-car-coming-out, why-doesn't-he-keep-his-eyes-on-the-road kind of trip. Among other things, a light rain had begun to fall, but we decided to go on to the circus anyway. After all, it would be dry under the tent, and we could still enjoy an interesting afternoon outing. When we finally arrived at the circus, and after leaving the car, my Mother threatened to kill me, if I ever got her into a car driven by Orvil again. During the circus, held in a typically large canvas tent, it began to rain even harder, and as the water began to saturate the tent, it began to drip down on the heads of all those who were trying to enjoy the circus. Mother pulled out her plastic raincap, and wore it during the rest of the performance that day. Orvil, not to be outdone, took out his large pocket-handkerchief, and after tying four little knots in the corners, proceeded to wear it over his baldhead for the rest of the show. Before long, he was getting as much attention as the circus performers, and about as many laughs as the paid clowns that day. As a driver, Orvil Reid truly established his own sort of reputation!"

Edith said there were many anecdotes about him and his fellow missionaries, many of which truly happened at annual mission meetings. She was quick to say, "Some of them may have been amplified over the years by imagination, but all of them tell us something more about Orvil Reid and the fellowship and relationship he enjoyed with the other missionaries."

She continued. "As you well know by now, Orvil had the ability most people have of talking much more than was necessary. With his interest in the goings-on of everything, and his desire to know all the reasons why and why not, he'd occasionally monopolize a meeting with his questions and comments. The Annual Mission Meeting of all the missionaries in Mexico was no exception. As a matter of fact, he looked forward to learning about everyone, and knowing all about their works and ministries. But once again, with something of a limited time-frame in which to report to one another, and make plans for the future, he became something of a friendly threat to completing the meeting within the designated time."

"Someone noticed that when Orvil had a book in his hand, he often became so involved in reading it that he did almost nothing else until he finished it, so at one particular mission meeting, Orvil began to read some new and absorbing book. It was not until the meeting was almost over that his fellow missionaries became aware that it had progressed so smoothly and so rapidly, without the usual Orvil Reid interrogations. Jokingly, they suggested in the somewhat humorous resolutions at the end of that meeting that someone be assigned to bring Orvil a new and interesting book each year. It was all said and done in love, but with a genuine and sincere intention behind it as well!

James Crane remembered another mission meeting anecdote. "There was the time when there was a desire to heighten the effect of a certain presentation at Mission Meeting. In order that the presentation might have a greater visual impact, someone was needed to represent the baby, or the baby Christian, or the baby missionary, just starting out in service. Orvil came up with the idea of his dressing up like a baby, and appearing during the presentation. It sounded good, but those others who were considering this, thought perhaps he'd appear wearing a big bib or a bonnet, or perhaps carrying a baby bottle or a large sucker. What they hadn't counted on was that Orvil would dress himself in nothing more than a diaper made of a sheet. Also, he didn't just appear and walk through the meeting hall during the presentation, he entered, and like the child he was portraying, climbed right up onto the piano bench, onto the piano keyboard, the music rack, and onto the top of the upright piano, where he sat and entertained them with childish faces and such actions as pretending to almost fall off a time or two. Now you have to remember that Orvil was a big human being. Not fat. But tall. And during those years, also muscular. So for him to do all this with a loosely fitted sheet pinned around him was something in itself. For most missionaries who were in attendance at that meeting, that is the one thing that seems to stand out in their memory of Orvil Reid at Mission Meeting.

Sitting close to Orvil as she was, Alma gave his head a gentle caress as she said, "Orvil genuinely loved and appreciated others who had served their Lord through years of missionary service. He honored one of them, our good friend, G.H. Lacy, in his poem, 'A Fellow Missionary.' Katie, I think you'll find it in that little book of his.

Fifty long years in the service of our Lord,
Living and preaching his Wonderful Word,
Always smiling, or singing a song,
Hunger and thirst, or perhaps an angry mob
Often came his way, yet he stayed at the job.

Through long trying war-days he faithfully worked,
Though life was in danger, he never once shirked.
A hammock, or the ground, a bed, or a cot,

236

He never once complained though hard was his lot.
Threatened by enemies, criticized by friends,
His only concern was the Gospel he defends.
Preacher, and teacher, counselor and friend,
In him a world of talents and virtues blend.

Eternity alone can ever hope to tell
The value of a life that is lived so well.
Influences set in motion will never die
Until all the ages of time pass by.
When God rewards his faithful when time shall end,
Bright will be the crown and the stars he will win.

Orvil spoke now. "Even though all of you have given me quite a roasting over these relationship with other missionaries, I value those times. I don't think I wrote my poem, 'To our Missionaries Emeritus' especially for any of you, but I think it fits in the conversation of the present time. I was probably not thinking at the time that in a few years I too would be included in this elect group. I always hoped my words might be a challenge to all who continue to serve where others have laid the missionary groundwork.

When times were dark and ranks were thin,
There were a faithful few
Who had the grace and grit to win,
And to the task be true.

We now are reaping where you sowed:
The torch, we took from you
Was carried o'er the roughest road
By you, friends, tried and true.

May we all now as faithful be,

As you were in your day,
Give faith and courage Lord, that we
May walk the same true way.

"After many years of service as a missionary in Mexico, and eleven months of mission service on five continents and in about thirty nations, I wrote another poem looking at 'Missions From A Retired Missionary's Point of View.' I think it will be a good one with which to end this session.

I think of the thousands of Christians living here,
and I am happy, yet sad,
I believe that none of them would willingly do bad,
But Satan is so cunning and sly,
That, to divert many from God's Will for their life he
will try.
He will try to make them flunk God's test,
Which is to give God their very best.
He may deceive some with a cunning "quirk,"
Getting them to the right place for the wrong work.
Or Satan may do a "right about face,"
And try to get them to do the right work in the wrong
place.

After being on the mission field over forty years,
When I hear a call for missionaries I still shed tears,
For, to start all over again, I'd like to go,
But the Foreign Mission Board says, "You're too old,
so it's no."
I am convinced that without any doubt,
Satan tries to keep missionaries from the most needy
fields out.
So he, many sincere people he tries to deceive,
Telling them that their homeland they should never
leave.

238

And not to give up high salaries, relatives, and familiar
security,
To waste their life in some neglected place across the
sea.
I have been in many countries of the world,
Where Christ's banner of salvation has never been
unfurled.
If I had a thousand lives, I want the Lord to know,
That, with each one of them, I would to some forgotten
field go.
Why should America, with less than a tenth
of the world's population,
Have nine-tenths of the lives, given to tell of Christ's
salvation?

Are we not willing affluence, relatives, and comforts to
leave,
That millions of lost souls salvation may receive?
Did our love-level for you Lord, to such a low-level
sag,
That to win millions of lost souls we put a material
price tag?
The very first point in a missionary call should be,
"Where in all the world, does the Lord need me?"
The next thing that a servant of the Lord should do,
Is ask, "What is the work, Lord, that you want me to
do?"

I could be wrong, but I really think that you,
If you pray and meditate about it, will think so too.
There are places where not one in a thousand has of
Christ heard,
And fewer still know the plan of salvation found in
God's Word.
Would you not say that the millions who of Christ
have never heard,
Should have priority in hearing God's Word?
I feel that to students, and to pastors, we should say,
Not "Why should you go?" but ask, "Why should you

stay?"

I challenge you to prayerfully take this test,
Then pray and leave to the Lord all the rest.
In one column, write all the reasons why you should go
To those whom without will never Christ know.
For there is no one there, them of Jesus to tell,
So, without you they are doomed to eternal hell.
On the other side, place the reasons why you should
stay:
Family, friends, and perhaps higher salary pay.

On fields where there are Christians on every block,
And there are radio and T.V. gospel messages around
the clock,
And the only reason most people to Christ do not go,
Is that they stubbornly refuse to do so.
Neither can we pray, "Lord, send others to the mission
field,
If we, to the Lord's call, are not willing to yield."
We, in our prayers cannot to the Lord honest be,
Unless we are willing to say, "Here am I Lord, send
me."

CHAPTER 19

THE FRIEND

After downing steaming-hot cups of Mexican-style cappuccino,

 they decided to move on to the subject of Orvil Reid, the Friend.

Kay was just starting the conversation by saying, "Orvil wore many hats, held many jobs," when Orvil reminded her, "Sombreros, Katie, sombreros."

"That's what I meant to say Orvil, that you wore many sombreros, and held many jobs. You had many titles, but the one which perhaps meant the most, was 'Orvil Reid, the Friend.' I know it embarrasses Orvil to hear it said, but his was a genuinely loving, giving spirit, which earned him that special recognition."

"Oh yes, he was a giving, generous person," Alma said, "almost to a fault. I remember what happened the day he took a day-trip to the Associational Camp. That particular morning, the Student Home cook reminded him of something he had almost forgotten, when she said, 'Oh Señor Reid, remember to take the pots from the kitchen. You know, the other señor said they never had enough to cook all the food. Just don't forget to bring them back. I will need them to prepare our own evening meal as well.'

"She helped him as he carefully loaded his car full of the large cooking pots from the student home kitchen. These weren't metal or stainless steel pots, but huge baked clay pots especially prepared for cooking large quantities of beans or rice.

"The meeting at the camp went well that day. Those in charge of preparing the food for the dozens of people who were in attendance appreciated the use of the pots for that extra big meal. Following the morning sessions, and the meal, he helped the kitchen crew wash the pots he had brought out from the Student Home, and he soon had them loaded back into his car for the return trip back into Guadalajara.

"Someplace on the highway that runs between the camp and the Student Home, he passed a group of 'the brothers' who had also left the meeting, and were trying to get a ride back into town. Being the kind of person he was, he stopped to give them a ride. In order to make room for the car-full of people, he had to rearrange some of the pots. When he got back to the Student Home, the cook there asked him, 'And Señor Reid, where are all the pots?'

"With nothing more than a slight and somewhat casual shrug of his shoulders, as if nothing significant had happened, he replied, 'Well, I was on the way home, when I passed this group of brothers waiting by the roadside for a ride back into town. When I realized that the car wasn't big enough for them and the pots, I had to make a decision. So we just unloaded the pots there on the side of the road, the people got in, and we all came on back.'

"And the pots?" she asked. "What happened to the pots?"

"Oh, I don't know. I'm not real sure," he replied, again somewhat nonchalantly. "We just left them there on the side of the highway. I'm sure someone has found them by now, and taken them home with them. Who knows Señora, maybe those people who found them needed them more than we did. Besides, we can always just get us some more."

"But I think not in time for me to prepare tonight's meal, Señor Reid. What do you think of that?"

His friend James Crane added, "To Orvil, people were always more important than pots!! He had a special place in his heart for people, and he hoped others would do the same as he expressed in his little poem, "We Need to Fall in Love."

We need to fall in love with the people,
We need to fall in love with God,
We need to think less of our church steeples,
And walk with folks like Jesus trod.

We need to fall in love with our calling,
To serve our God and fellowman,
For whitened harvest's needs are appalling,

243

And soon, we'll end our brief life's span.

Kay recalled some of those special people Orvil had fallen in love with. "Yes, Brother Orvil had a very special place in his heart for people, especially widows and orphans. He became a special friend to many families following the death of the pastor-husband and father. Three of those families were the Rodriguez, the Jimenez, and the Hernandez families. They had some interesting things to say about *Hermano* Orvil.

"The death of Bro. Rodriguez in the nearby state of Michoacan left a widow and a family of six children. During those years, there was not much help available for pastor's families. Orvil had such a heart for people that he found a couple of ways to help them. Omar, the middle child in that family remembered the first time he ever saw Orvil Reid.

"He arrived in what seemed to me to be an enormous car, the biggest one he had ever seen." Kay added, "It was probably Orvil's old carry-all station wagon, which, in the eyes of little Omar Rodriguez WAS the biggest car he'd ever seen. As impressed as Omar was with the car, it was not the car that left the strongest memory with Omar. He said Hermano Orvil knew what children everywhere seemed to love; so on the outskirts of town, he had bought a stack of the biggest, ripest watermelons he had ever seen. Without saying almost anything, Orvil began to unload them outside the Rodriguez house. Omar recalls it with these words:

"My Daddy had recently died. We had already been told we were going to have to move from the house where we were living. We didn't know what we were going to do. The six of us children and my mother were all a bit scared and more than a little confused by all that was going on, and here without warning, or announcement, or seemingly, without much of a reason, this very tall, almost bald American man, wearing a big smile, with his hair sticking out from the sides of his head, drove up in a big car and was now standing in my yard holding out his arms full of watermelons to us. He may not have known how scared we were, but he knew how much we needed some definite expression of love. And he knew exactly how to win that love. What child could resist that kind of treat! We couldn't. From that day on, Orvil Reid was more than a foreigner, more than an American, more than a stranger. He became our friend. Whatever happened after that, or whatever didn't, it would always be over-shadowed by that 'image' of that caring missionary."

Kay continued. "It wasn't long before Orvil helped the Rodriguez family in another way. When they did have to move from the pastorium where they were living, he helped them acquire a small plot of land. Orvil had also acquired a small manually operated machine-press for making bricks. Omar can hardly recall exactly how it worked, but he remembers that Orvil showed him and his brothers how to mix the ingredients for bricks, put them into the machine, press them down, form them into the right size, and release them. After a time of drying, they had something like concrete-block-like bricks, which they used to build their very own house. Again, Orvil the Friend was right where he needed to be, doing exactly what he needed to do to help. Again though, he didn't DO the work, he taught them how to do it. What can others learn from that?

"Another family that Orvil helped during a difficult time was the

Jimenez family. Señora Jimenez remembers Orvil Reid this way."

"I first became acquainted with Señor Reid, when he and a group of young people from the student home came to my area of Mexico for a spiritual retreat. Quila, where I lived, was a couple of hours away in the mountains that surrounded Guadalajara. They had invited some of the young people of our area to join them. We all took whatever food we could, and we spent the days studying the Bible and talking about God and life. At night, they led us in services with singing, testimonies and preaching.

"We slept wherever we could that night as there were no facilities for sleeping. The next day, following a morning of activities, we all went home. As much as I enjoyed the fellowship at the retreat, I was sad because I so wanted to leave Quila and study in Guadalajara. Señor Reid learned about my wanting to go there, so I was invited to come to Guadalajara shortly thereafter, and continue my studies. My main reason for not going before was that I had no place to stay, and I certainly couldn't afford to rent a room. Señor Reid and Señorita Miriam McCullough arranged for me to live in the Girl's Student Home, so I continued to be a part of Bro. Reid's 'family.'

"Señor Reid stayed in touch with me over the following years even after I married and had a family of eight children myself. For some years, my husband pastored in Michoacan and in Tuxpa, then later in the oceanside community of Manzanillo, where we were living when he was diagnosed with throat cancer. I didn't know what we were going to do when he got so sick. We went to Guadalajara where my husband received treatment at the Mexican American Hospital, but he

always wanted to go back to Manzanillo so he could

preach on Sundays. His health got so bad, and the cancer spread so rapidly that he could hardly talk, but still he wanted to preach. Bro. Orvil helped him get a microphone where he would be able to preach, even when he couldn't speak above a whisper. Almost until the days before he died, he was still preaching the gospel. When he died in the Hospital, I didn't know how we were going to survive. I guess no one ever prepares well for the death of their husband and the father of their family. We certainly didn't. But again, Señor Reid was there. Somehow, he arranged for us to acquire a small house in Guadalajara. I think maybe it was taken as a payment for a bill following the death of some other man in the hospital. We moved there, and my family and I continued to receive the blessing of having the Reids as our friends for many more years.

"Hermano Orvil began to use our yard as one of the meeting-places for the children. Of course, with my eight, he already had a good-sized group to start with. He'd gather them around out in the street in front of the house, and start to play with them, doing tricks with coins, or displays of strength, or playing games, or singing. He'd already told my children to invite some of their friends, which they always did, for Señor Reid was a lot of fun to have around. Boys and girls of all ages grew to love him, and grew to know and love the Lord whom he told them about. In the lives of all the Jimenez family, he truly lived up to that title given him by many people, that of being...a friend!"

"Another family that Orvil helped was the Molina family. During the years when no pastor had his own car, many used the buses, including the pastor-father of this family who rode a bicycle. One afternoon as he was doing his visiting on his bicycle, the automobile of a teen-age driver accidentally hit him. After several agonizing days in the hospital, he died, leaving a wife and ten children, ages two to eighteen, without help.

Moises, the oldest son in the family, now a successful Christian businessman, wrote how surprisingly so many needs were met following this tragedy.

"At first I thought how can we do this? With so many younger brothers and sisters, I'll probably have to go to work to help support the family. Of course, after several months, we could no longer live in the parsonage. The father of the girl involved in the accident gave us a small lot and Bro. Reid somehow helped us have a small house.

"He and other pastors and church people continued to bring food and necessary things to our house. It seemed to me that we always had something to eat, until that one day when there were no more beans in the kitchen, no more tortillas, and the rice and coffee was all but used up. There was nothing left to eat. I asked my mother, 'What are we going to do now?'

"She answered me, 'We will do what we have always done.'

"As the hour for the noon meal approached, I became more and more apprehensive. I was surprised when she began to set the table. This surprise turned to frustration for me as she called all of us to the table, and she asked us to bow our heads and thank the Lord for 'our food.' I found my surprise turning to anger, although I knew I could take this; I was just concerned about how this was going to affect my younger brothers and sisters. She asked us to bow our heads and close our eyes as she said the prayer of blessing. I found I could bow my head, but I could not close my eyes. I just stared down at that empty plate and bowl.

"She had no more than said the 'amen' to her prayer, than there was a muffled sound of a knock at our door, like someone hitting it with their arm or shoulder. We opened the door to find Hermano Reid standing there with his large hands full of sacks of rice and beans. As he brought his sacks into the kitchen, he said to us boys, 'Go out to my car and bring in the rest.' As I was carrying in a case of fresh fruit, my repentant heart then acknowledged again my mother's faith, and I never again doubted that God does provide for us.

My mother never really said too much about my attitude that night, but I learned a great deal about having faith that night. Hermano Orvil was not God in any sense of the word, but his arrival that day, served to remind us all of the need to wait on the Lord, and to depend on Him whenever things got so desperate that we couldn't see the way through the unbelievably tough times that come in our lives."

Alma told us how Orvil dedicated his book, *The Challenge Of Mexico To Missions*, "to friends everywhere." He could have easily written the poem, "He Is A Friend," about himself – something he would never have done. Yet, it seems so appropriate.

As fresh, cool springs and pretty flowers
Make light the traveler's weary hours,
Who treads the desert hot and bare,
A real true friend who understands
Is like an oasis in the sands
That fills the pilgrim's heart with cheer.

His worth cannot be told in gold
Who cheers some weary, burdened soul,
And helps him on his lonely way,
Yet he who lightens others' cares
And helps to dry another's tears
Has made his own a brighter day.

The shriveled soul who seeks his own,
Who thinks of self and self alone,
Will live a miser's life at best,
While he who serves his fellowman

251

By doing all the good he can
Has found at last true happiness!

CHAPTER 20

THE LATER YEARS

Excerpts from a couple of the more recent Christmas newsletters, which Orvil and Alma continued to send to their friends each year, allow us a glimpse into some of their near-retirement-year activities.

"Christmas Newsletter from The Reids, 1973: Oh to be a new missionary again and to have the thrill of putting into practice in future years, all the ideas and plans of the August Mission meeting! With only one year left to serve in Mexico, we comfort ourselves with the thought that we will never retire. In a different way, in a different place, we will be working with new ideas and methods -- thrilling adventures still before us."

"Christmas Newsletter from The Reids, 1974: Dr. Billy Graham's wife, Ruth said that the hardest thing missionaries have to do is to say goodbye. Thirty-six years ago for Orvil, and thirty-one for Alma, we said goodbye to loved ones in the states to come to Mexico; now it is time to say goodbye here. This will be the last newsletter written from Mexico.

"One afternoon during the recent Mission meeting, business was put aside, and there was a surprise party for the Reids, loving words from fellow missionaries, gifts from different sections of the country: a famous handmade Aztec calendar; a book of fifty-nine plates of Mexican art in full color, another book, a sunset pictorial of Mexico, wooden sculpture of a Seri Indian from Sonora, a typical Indian doll, black pottery from Oaxaca, and a set of hand-painted dishes from Guadalajara. Missionaries Bill and Pinky Gray even 'wrote a book;' a Book of Letters from friends everywhere, including the

Foreign Mission Board, and Mexico Mission president James Crane presented a genuine sheepskin scroll from the Mission; a big cake and other refreshments and special singing followed."

And on the back cover of that issue was their "Prayer Of Thanksgiving."

Thank you dear Lord, that you called us to go,
And serve you these years in Old Mexico.
All thirty-six years, you walked by our side,
Our Lord and Savior, our Strength and Guide.

Thank you that thousands of souls have been saved,
For lives you set free that sin had enslaved.
For national pastors, and humble folk
Who faithfully served, though heavy the yoke.

For missionaries who left all to come
To work with great zeal, that they might win some.
For those at home, who stayed in the breach,
That we missionaries might go out and preach.

Through their prayers and gifts, our Lord has used them
To share in all things that we did for him.
For Cooperative Program, and Lottie Moon funds,
Their lifeline to all of our mission field runs.

For our mission Board, from the depth of our heart,
Thanks, for each member did more than his part.
The Board shares our sorrows, and victories, too,
And shows deep concern for all that we do.

For so many blessings Lord, thanks from our heart;
But the task is not done -- we've just made a start.
Thrust forth more laborers, the harvest is white,
And millions seem doomed to eternal night.

God make us willing to suffer and die.
We are just creeping -- Lord, help us to fly!
Set us afire with a burning zeal:
Help us the tragedy of lost souls to feel.

May we give all Lord; may we never shirk
For soon comes the night when no man can work.

"Wasn't it about this time when you continued doing some of your strong-man feats?" Don asked.

"Oh yes. My endurance tests didn't stop when we left for the states that last time. I continued giving demonstrations during a couple of short-term mission trips to other countries, as well as during our final furlough, right up to the service in which we were to be officially retired. Most of those who were scheduled to retire that year were delighted that the Foreign Mission Board was willing to fly them into the Washington D.C. airport, then transport them down to Richmond in rented cars. Not me. I decided to make one last mark in the Foreign Missionary Book of Records. I decided not to take the plane, the bus, or the car. I decided to run the 550 miles, all the way from The Home Mission Board in Atlanta to the Foreign Mission Board in Richmond."

The Baptist Press Report released the news in the Sept. 8, 1976 edition of THE BAPTIST STANDARD in the following way:

"Orvil W. Reid, 68-year-old missionary to Mexico will jog from the Home Mission Board in Atlanta Sept. 3 on the first lap of a 550-mile 'Run for Life.' During appearances along the way to Richmond, he hopes to win 1,000 people to Christ, and collect at least $60,000 for U.S. and world relief. He plans to reach the Foreign Mission Board in Richmond by Oct. 11. That's the date when he and his wife, Alma, will officially retire after 38 years' missionary service.

"Each retiring missionary receives a bonus, and the Reids have already pledged $1,000 of theirs as a contribution to suffering people of the world. Like other proceeds from the run, the contribution will be divided, with 60 percent going to world relief through the Foreign Mission Board and 40 percent to needs in the United States through the Home Mission Board. Reid will receive nothing for his run. Friends are underwriting his expenses.

"Executive Director Arthur B. Rutledge of the Home Mission Board will offer a prayer of dedication as Reid starts his run down auxiliary roads at I-85 and along U.S. 29 through Georgia, South Carolina and North Carolina to Richmond. The lean and wiry missionary will jog about 20 miles a day, five days a week. At rallies in churches, schools, prisons, stadiums and other locations, Reid will challenge youth and others to clean living to acceptance of Christ as Savior, and to commitment to the will of God."

"Alma and I took that one thousand dollars mentioned in the press release from our savings, and sent a dollar each to a thousand churches, that were on our mailing list, encouraging them to use it to start their offering for world hunger. It worked! Many people wrote back, sharing how that had motivated them personally or their church to become more involved in giving to World Hunger. A sixty year-old businessman in one church where I spoke told how receiving that dollar had changed not only his planned giving, but also that of his church. He said, 'Brother Reid, I want you to know that I gave a thousand dollars more than I had planned on giving for world hunger, because of that one dollar you sent to us.'"

"A Tennessee pastor told me some time later that he was a member of the State Executive Committee. He shared how they had talked a lot about world hunger in their meeting. He went on to say, 'We talked about your jog, and for the first time in history, we voted as a

257

state, to give a hundred thousand dollars for world hunger, and your jog and your emphasis had much to do with that decision.'"

"I was sure my Run for Life would be a good way to put a strong finish to my Missionary Career. Boys from the Royal Ambassador organizations in various Baptist churches of Atlanta and Richmond, as well as RA's from all those churches in between would run with me. Some might even carry the American flag, while some would run with the Christian flag. And just like in the Olympics, some would run the race with a torch. Instead of these things symbolizing the Olympic spirit, they would stand for Christians holding forth the Banner of the Word, and running the race, finishing the course, and holding forth the light of the world. At the same time, World Hunger would benefit from charitable donations given all along the way. On the run, I preached and talked to over 18,800 people, many of who made recorded decisions for Christ. I led services and gave demonstrations of his physical strength in 38 churches, 18 schools, 10 prisons, 8 rallies, and 3 children's homes."

"This Run for Life" not only caught the attention of the religious press writers, but the secular press in many of the cities where I ran, and gave my special talks and demonstrations as well. I think Alma has an entire folder of those press-clippings somewhere around here. Read them and use any you want to."

Larry Kilman, writer for News Daily, wrote in the August 29, 1976 Daily Recorder Sunday Magazine, an article titled A SHOW OF STRENGTH, which read in part:

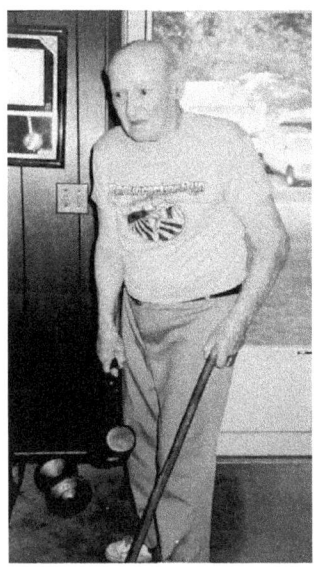

"Reid's performance didn't come about overnight. He has garnered most of his strong-man feats from where you would expect to find them -- the circus. "Every few years or so I hear about a new trick," explains Reid. "The first one came from a circus performer in Guadalajara. The man put an anvil on his stomach and someone hit it with a sledgehammer. He would sing afterward. I started with someone hitting softer, then harder, and harder. I found I could take it as hard as they could give it. Instead of singing afterward, I sing while they do it. Reid also went one step further than one circus performer in Germany. 'I watched a circus performer in Germany being choked with a rope. I do it too, only I sing or recite verses. The problem with it is that the blood to my head is cut off because the veins are right under the skin, and I can pass out. I found that the time it takes to sing 'Auld Lang Syne' or 'Happy Birthday' is about all the time I have.'

Sarah Holeman wrote in her account called RETIRING

MISSIONARY JOGS FROM ATLANTA TO RICHMOND, in the

September 25, 1976 issue of The Durham Sun:

"My miles are longer than other people's," he said. He explained that he could clock his own distance by a system of counting breaths. "One breath equals four running steps, and 100 breaths equals one finger," he says. Counting off all ten fingers means that two and a half miles have been run and then every two and a half miles are marked off by the transfer of a twig from one pocket to another. I can think while I'm running" he said, "but I can't talk. This keeps my mind occupied and keeps me from getting bored."

Steve Knowlton, Staff Writer for "The Raleigh (N.C.) Time"

headlined his column of Sept. 28, 1976, ORVIL'S ANTICS BLEND

SHOW AND MISSION. Part of what he wrote was:

"Huffing his way up the Beltline, 68-year-old Orvil Reid almost blends in with the construction crews which line the superhighway...but a glance at the shiny

260

bald head poking above the elastic sweatband shows him to be past retirement age for hard labor. Orvil Reid is doing what he does nearly every day of his life. He is jogging for Jesus. An energetic man whose machinegun-fire speech is so rapid, it is often indistinct, Reid is on an Atlanta-to-Richmond jaunt...an aging Elmer Gantry with indefatigable energy."

And Orvil himself wrote, following the run:

"I ran to say to children and young people how they could easily get off the hook of cigarettes, alcohol and drugs and begin now to prepare for healthy lives. I ran for senior citizens, to say they don't have to sit around and wait for death when they get to retirement age. I ran for people to be aware of the world hunger problem. But more than anything else, I ran with the hope of helping people to have eternal life and to dedicate their lives to the cause of Christ. So my motives were strong enough to keep me going in the rain, the cold and the heat. I would crawl from New York City to Los Angeles on my knees, if I knew one person would come to know Christ."

And in their Christmas newsletter, 1976, he summed up the jog as

he wrote:

"The thought that I was crazy and should act my age came many time to this sixty-eight year old missionary as I ran in preparation for, and during the jog from the Home Mission Board, Atlanta, to the Foreign Mission Board, Richmond. Preparation began Dec. 1, 1975 through Sept. 2, 1976, during which time I jogged 2300 miles. The jog of 550 miles began Sept 3, and ended Oct. 11. The thrill of breaking the Welcome Orvil ribbon at the Foreign Mission Board, and knowing how God had used the effort to glorify Him, will remain.

261

"There were 78 services and program in schools, prisons, children's homes, and churches. Three hundred confessed Christ as Savior; several thousand promised to give up harmful habits and be faithful in stewardship. We do not know the amount given for world disaster relief, (the total was later revealed to be over $100,000 dollars), but are sure many lives will be saved."

Whether "The Jog of Life" was written during those days or not,

it certainly seems appropriate to place it here in the chronology of

things.

Life's tasks are like a jog that you might do,
It takes both faith and grit to get you through,
To climb a steep hill may cause you to frown,
But each step up means one step going down.
It's not the downgrade that will make you fit,
But the steep hill that makes you want to quit.
Just to coast down never brings the thrill
That comes when you conquer a man-sized hill.
It does little good to idle along,
You have to push some to make your heart strong.
Dogs bark, rain falls, and it may even snow,
But you step up the pace, and on you go.
When you reach your home, you are feeling fine,
And in your heart, you can feel the sunshine.
We'll keep on jogging with the jogging band,
And jog together in the Promised Land.
We'll receive our "patch" for a well-run race,
Rewards come for works, we are saved by grace.

As a reminder not only of that particular "jog for life," but of years of "running for the Lord," and a lifetime of dedicated service, one of Orvil's jogging shoes from that historic run was given to his college alma mater, Oklahoma Baptist University, and the other is on display with missionary memorabilia at the Foreign Mission Board. Perhaps many who see those shoes will never know the person who wore it, or know much about the life behind the man, but perhaps someone will be inspired to continue to "run the good race and finish the course."

"You've heard it said, Don, that those in the Old West wanted to die with their boots on. I'd be happy to die with my jogging shoes on, especially if I were trying to help one person live a healthier, more fruitful life. Only God knows how many people did not die for lack of food, or medical care, because one 69-year old great grandfather cared enough to jog 550 miles for world hunger, and emphasized giving to that worthy cause all along the way. Not only did the money come in, but also dozens of souls were won, and many young people came forward dedicating their lives to world missions. I have tried to be faithful to the proclamation of His message even to my retirement service as a Foreign Missionary. They may not all run from one state to another, but how I wish all missionaries everywhere could learn something of the same."

It took many years before Orvil and Alma began to slow down, although they have been retired more years than some folks even serve as missionaries. They seemed to have only a few requirements for a retirement location: that it be near old friends, that it be near old places, that it be near a church where they could continue to serve and be active, and that it be near a fitness center where Orvil could continue staying in shape.

All of those requirements were met when they located a small house just off the edge of the Southwestern Seminary campus in Ft. Worth, Texas. Many of their old friends were active or emeritus faculty members there. They had both attended Seminary there, so felt at home in that part of the country. There was a generous sprinkling of churches all around them. And Orvil could go the Seminary Fitness Center any time and every time he wanted to. And Alma could enjoy fixing up their small house just the way she had always wanted to do. Everything seemed just perfect.

And it was. Orvil began compiling his writings, and even doing some writing and rewriting his own memoirs. They became active members of a nearby church, and were soon involved in all the activities of the church and the seminary that time and energy would allow for. Everything really did seem just perfect.

There had been a day a year or so before when they weren't so sure it would ever be good again. That was the day when Orvil suffered a stroke that initially left him completely paralyzed on his left side. Alma briefly described what had happened in the following way in a letter she wrote to the Mexico Mission some months later.

"Most of you know about Orvil being a jogger. He is on another kind of 'jog' now, one far more important than any of the others. But Dr. Eugene Greer, Texas State Missions Commission, who was the coordinator of Orvil's jog from Atlanta to Richmond jog back in 1976 is with him all the way, cheering him on to his goal of complete recovery.

"This run began January 28 when Orvil was hospitalized with a stroke. What a surprise when Dr. Jose Gonzalez, our Mexican 'son' who lived with us in Mexico, who happened to be in Dallas just one day, the day of the stroke, answered my phone call that night. Orvil, who never gets sick, not even a headache, had had a stroke. After three weeks in the hospital, two weeks in the rehabilitation center, and now in outpatient therapy, Orvil continues the run with faith and determination.

"We had come to Dallas in January to be there just a month, and then planned to move on to other Texas cities, in a special mission work project, planned by the Texas Missions Department, in cooperation with the Home Mission Board. Orvil had worked hard in Texas, as he had last year during our seven months in Africa and Europe.

"Orvil is getting along fine. We thank you for telephone calls, visits, flowers, cards, letters,   and other manifestations of your love and concern. These have come from all over the United States and foreign countries. Thank you for your prayers."

In an Editorial in the March 9, 1978 "Oklahoma Baptist Messenger," Jack L. Gritz also wrote about that

265

interesting sideline concerning Dr. Gonzalez being in Dallas on that particular night.

"During his early days at Guadalajara long ago, Orvil Reid took in a 12-year-old boy who had no place to go, nothing to eat, no place to sleep at night, named Jose Gonzalez. Reid asked Jose to come and live in a student home he had started. The boy worked, went to school, and graduated from the medical school of the University of Guadalajara.

"As a physician, he specialized as an internist and cardiologist. A few days ago the 69-year-old Reid suffered a stroke while visiting in Dallas. His wife Alma, thought to herself, 'Oh, if only Jose Gonzalez were here.' She picked up the phone and called Dr. E. Lamar Cole whom they knew because of his interest in missions. But it was not Dr. Cole who answered the phone. The man who answered was Dr. Gonzalez. He had come to Dallas to visit Dr. Cole. The two doctors rushed to the aid of their stricken friend. Within a few minutes, Reid was in a hospital. He is undergoing therapy for his paralyzed left arm and doing well."

Orvil says, "When I regained consciousness, I couldn't move my left arm and leg at all. I had plenty of strength, but I just wasn't plugged in. When you have a stroke you feel like a thing, not a person. That stroke changed a lot of things. But it didn't whip me completely down. In compiling his writings, I found strength in some of my own words written years before in a small collection titled *A Bouquet For You*.

No matter what hardships or dangers assail,
And though health, wealth, friends, and everything fail,
A man can brave storms and conquer the tide,
For one's never whipped till he's whipped inside!

266

Though bruised and bleeding, and cast to the ground,
He'll come up for more, you can't keep him down,
Though weakened and worn, his time will he bide,
A man's never whipped till he's whipped inside!

Though enemies mock, and friends may betray,
He'll last the long night and win the new day,
He holds to the truth all great men have tried,
A man's never whipped till he's whipped inside!

"I was never whipped inside, yet during the months and years following my stroke, it was more and more difficult for me to write and do some of those simple things I was doing before. I couldn't run for a while, and when I was able to jog again I felt like I was carrying a 300-pound man on my back now. I was in a wheelchair for three months, then had a walker and crutches and later used a cane.

Alma recalls one day "when we were walking out in the woods, he just picked up his cane and started jogging. I began going along with him to be sure he wouldn't fall. Time allows everyone to heal somewhat. Even Orvil Reid!! His philosophy of life is based on Romans 8:28: Nothing can happen to you that the Lord won't make work for good."

Some highlights from Christmas editions of their Newsletters

since their "retirement," let their readers know that they were continuing their mission trips and activities during these years, even though they weren't doing so in Mexico.

"In 1977, we spent 7 months in Africa and Europe speaking, preaching and singing." Even during those working-retirement years, Orvil still had a genuine interest in ' Search for The Will of Our Lord as he wrote in that same newsletter.

Lord, you have a plan for each child of thine:
There is a task, a time, and a place.
Our only desire is to know thy will,
Lead us by your wisdom and grace.

There are many places where we could serve,
Some far away, and others close,
But, of all the places, you know the one
Where our lives can serve Thee the most.

Some things Lord, Thou knowest, could lead us astray:
Comfort, money, vanity, pride,
But deep in our hearts, we only would do
The will of Him, who for us dies.

Reveal unto us Thine own, perfect will,
Show us what Thou wantest us to do.
Then give us the love, the wisdom and power,
That we, to Thy will may be true.

"In 1979, we returned to Guadalajara for a year, working in evangelistic and lay-training work." This was just a couple of years after Orvil's stroke. He wrote in that newsletter, "When I awoke from that stroke, I had a wonderful feeling that if I had died, I would have been with the Lord, but He seemed to shout, 'No, there is too much work to do!'

"In 1980, maybe the Rambling Reids will settle down for awhile, for they are buying a house. With a big seminary library and the aerobics center nearby, Orvil says we are about as near heaven as we can get on this earth.

"In 1984, our big event was a mission trip to Mexico for another four months, and a partnership trip last month.

"In 1987, forty-four years ago, we sent our first newsletter from Mexico. Now, near 80, I know that my life is far spent, but many a race has been won in the home-stretch sprint. In spite of my stroke nine years ago, when I had to learn to walk and talk again, I am thankful that my influence with young people is as great now as ever. We attend chapel services and other programs at the seminary. At church we are as active as we can be. We are working on two books, and Orvil reads one book a week, and writes a poem daily."

Some of his poems took on a decidedly different approach during these "senior years," such as the following, "A Neighborly Plea to My Fellow Older Adults."

Let us not waste our beautiful autumn years
By magnifying our doubts and our fears.
To be sure, we can always find some pain, if we are
alert,
But let's think of our many parts we have that never
hurt.
Let us not major on grieving for what we have not,
But let us thank our dear Lord for the things we've got.

Let's pray to God that we will never forget
That, as is the beauty of sunrise, so is the sunset!
To think of death as the end of life is a great sin,
When God tells us that, then a greater life will
begin.

269

Then, we'll take a trip by God's wonderful grace,
And visit all the stars and planets of outer space.
We will thrill as we visit the most beautiful stars,
For, as heirs of our Lord, all those places will be ours.

Before I had a paralyzing stroke,
MILES of jogging I would make,
Now, I praise my Lord for each step I can still take.
Let us not only of the negative possibilities of life
surmise,
But still look for the rainbow, and beautiful clouds in
the skies.
This old age saying should have a great lesson for you
and me,
"Many people are blind, because they refuse anything
to see!"

Fellow Senior Adults, sad surely will be your life's fate,
If you, socially begin to withdraw and to hibernate,
Very soon, one will be lonely and fellowship with
friends will lack,
But if one seeks others to love truly, then many will love
him back.
Our friends and relatives are passing on day by day,
And unless we seek other friends, we'll be lonely on
life's way.
But, let us not seek friends with a purely selfish desire,
But that we may bless others and help them to inspire,
For when we share friendship with another, sad and
alone,
Then a great blessing comes not only to others' hearts,
but to our own.

And the truth of God's promise, to all will prove to be
true,
When God tells us, Give, and truly it will be given unto
you."
(Luke. 6:38)

270

Their lifestyle is a simpler one now. Just the kind most folks wish they had the liberty to enjoy. I'm sure whatever else Orvil would say about this part of his life, he would still agree with the idea expressed in his poem written many years before, "I Am A Multimillionaire."

Who says I am poor, cannot be aware
Of all the great wealth that is mine.
The gold of the sunset, the clouds so fair,
The vines that about me entwine.

The sweet-scented air from the new-mown hay,
The gentle perfume of the flowers,
The melodies of the songbirds so gay,
The castles of pines with their towers.

The waters that sing in the rippling brook,
Or shout in the waves of the sea,
The hills and dales, and the cozy nook
Are filled with rich treasures for me.

My millions of diamonds shine in the dews,
My sapphires all glow in the sky,
My cloud-pearls sparkle in dazzling hues,
Such wealth no man's money can buy.

The wealth of all nature, so great and dear,
To even the poorest is free,
So, all nature's beauties I see and hear
Are part of the gifts God gives me.

The couple of weeks with the Reids ended too soon for Don and Kay, but they had to get back to the mountains of New Mexico. There was work to do, Kay as a nurse at the hospital, and Don had pages of notes to read and a

271

stack of tapes to transcribe. It was hard to leave the Reids, for these had been special days together.

They said their goodbyes at the same place they'd said their hellos just a few days ago. Mexican abrazo-hugs and handshakes started in the living room. As Don and Kay went onto the porch, there were more goodbyes. Orvil and Alma followed them outside, where in the driveway, in the shade of that front-yard tree, there was yet another round of hugs and handshakes and thank-you's, and please come again. Don and Kay took one last glimpse back as they drove away and saw Alma and Orvil standing on that small porch waving until they were well out of sight. They stood there in silence for a moment, then Alma turned to Orvil and said, "Well, it's back to being just the two of us now."

Orvil replied, "That's the way it's been for a good long time now, and I wouldn't want it any other way. Where's my hat? I think I'll go for a little walk."

Orvil and Alma lived there as long as they could. Plants continued to grow in pots in every available place in the house. Memories and keepsakes of their years of life and service in Mexico remained on their walls. Orvil could still talk your ear off. Especially when he began to reminisce about his favorite topic -- Mexico. His descriptive talk became a little more rambling than it was some years ago, but it is was no less beautiful and impressive as he spoke with such loving fervor of "his neighbor to the south."

"Mexico is a good place to rest. The rush and hurry of life is not noticed so much. The people take time to live, to be friends, and to enjoy life. Our neighbor to the south is a land of contrasts. Men, burros, oxen, and horses may be seen carrying their heavy loads: while modern cars, buses, and trains whiz by and airplanes zoom overhead. In one field you will see people plowing with oxen hitched to crooked-stick plows, while others are harvesting grain with hand scythes, or trading out the grain with oxen or burros, all as in the days of Ruth in biblical times. Just around a mountain you may see modern tractor farming and new threshers rolling out the golden grain.

"You will see primitive Indians who live much as they did centuries ago: you will also come to know men of business, science and culture with a polish that is found only among the Latin races.

"You can choose your climate any time of the year. In winter, you are never over a few hours from warm sunny weather, where outdoor bathing is in season all the year. Or if you are fleeing from the heat, you are never far from the mountains where on the hottest night you will need a thin blanket to sleep comfortably. For instance, a half-hour drive from Mexico City will take you near the perennial snow, or it will take you where the tropical flowers grow all the year round.

"You may fish for trout in the rushing streams, for white fish in the lakes, or if you prefer deep-sea fishing, you may find a school of shark, sailfish, or others. Perhaps you like to hunt for big game or small. You will find Mexico always inviting you to adventure and fun.

"If you like to study prehistoric man in his haunts, the archeological ruins of the Toltecs, the great pyramid to the sun and to the moon, the "city of the Gods" near Mexico City, the Maya ruins in Oaxaca and

Chiapas, and many other places invite you to turn back the pages of history many, many centuries. Once we camped on a hunting trip in the midst of dozens of Indian mounds where there had been altars to heathen gods, and broken bits of prehistoric pottery were found everywhere.

"If you are a mountain climber, the eternal snowcapped peaks of the volcanos, the Sleeping Woman and the Mountain that Smokes near Mexico City, or the Pico de Orizaba near Veracruz, dare you to reach the opening to the endless pits of their craters.

"Best of all about Mexico is to know the people. It has been our pleasure to eat and sleep in the palm and bamboo home of the most humble Mexican, to visit also in the home of such people as an ex-state Governor, who is an example of culture and refinement; in the home of a nephew of a late President, and to be thrilled by his stories of the Mexican Revolution; also to sit in the home of the mother of one of the Presidents of Mexico, while she opened her heart about problems that she wanted to share with her Christian brethren.

"To know our Mexican people is to love them. When you understand their problems and the hardships that have been theirs through the centuries, you will admire them because of the progress they have made against such odds. Much of their history has been lived in political, economic, and religious slavery. Other nations were enriched by the political, economic, and even religious exploitation of the people.

"More than any material need you will be touched by the spiritual need of Mexico. You will be impressed by the deeply religious nature of the people, by the towering cathedrals with their altars overlaid with gold. You will see people going up stone walks on bare knees to pour out their hearts in supplication, as their arms are outstretched toward a cold stone image that is deaf to their pleas, blind to their tears, and cannot feel the kisses that are the expressions of hungry hearts reaching out after God. Your heart will ache when you know that not many of the millions of Mexico has ever had a Bible of New Testament in his hands, nor even heard of the new birth, without which no one can see God."

About this time, Alma, who had been patiently sitting close by, or had been desperately trying to get a word in edgewise herself, would begin to think that Orvil had talked on long enough, although the fascinated visitor could probably listen to him talk on and on. Yet, as the loving wife she still was, she will still get in enough of a good "rising inflection Orrr-villlle" for him to realize it himself, and bring his reminiscing conversation to a quick stopping place, only to have it continue the very next time someone would sit down with him long enough to allow him to begin it all over again.

Sitting in their living room, hearing them talk about their wonderful life together, listening to Orvil recount those experiences that happened years before that continue to add richness to years that abound in the kind of wealth some of us only wish we had, one suspects that what Orvil wrote about "Life" many years ago in that little collection, *Anchors For Life's Storms*, was as true for them today as it was when it was written.

> *Life is giving and taking,*
> *Life is blessings and cares,*
> *Life is sleeping and waking,*
> *Life is smiling and tears.*

Life is righting and wronging,
Life's an investment that pays,
Life is dreading and longing,
Life is knowing and praise.

Life is loving and hating,
Life is a gain and a loss,
Life is progress and waiting,
Life is a crown and a cross.

Life is gladness and sorrow,
Life is beauty and pain,
Life's a today and tomorrow,
Life is a goal to attain.

Life is laughing and crying
Life is sunshine and rain,
Life is living and dying,
Dying, then living again.

All in the life of the liver
Must blend to make up the whole,
Life is a gift from the Giver,
A beautifying of the soul!

Knowing all we know about the early years, the griefs, the struggles, as well as what we know about Orvil Reid the Fieldman, Orvil Reid the Missionary, Orvil Reid the Printer, the Strongman, the Romantic, and the Student Worker, we know much about his inner attitude concerning life. As he expresses in the thoughts of the very first lines of his poem, "How Old Are You?" mere years can never make one old. Orvil and Alma Reid are far from being old, and I think it's another Orvil Reid poem, which applies to them now as much as it ever has.

As he begins to quote it, Alma moves to sit on the arm of his padded recliner chair. She gently takes his hand, looks lovingly into his eyes, and smiles, knowing that she will likely have to prompt him from time to time.

Stay young! Mere years can never make one old:
In all mankind youth's fount is found.
Age comes when spirits shrivel and grow cold,
When life with selfish fears is bound.

When one begins to live within himself,
And lives too much within the past,
When too much thought concerns his state of health,
Don't count his years, he's old at last.

Keep growing, and learn something new each day,
Look not behind, look straight ahead,
Fill every day with work, with prayer and play,
And worry not for drink or break.

For worry kills more folk than work, or plagues,
Anger and grudges take their toll.
Though weak in body and covered with rags,
Spring's sun can shine within the soul.

Do not forget the body's not the man.
It is his humble house of clay,
His earthly dwelling place through life's brief span,
One brief stop, then he goes his way.

When they first settled down in Ft. Worth, Orvil had the idea of trying to read most of the books in the library at the Seminary, but with the new library building, there were going to be over a million books and periodicals, so he gave up hope of reading them all before the end of the century. By that time, he says, "I won't have Dr.

277

Scarborough, Dr. Dana, Dr. Copeland, Dr. Maston and Dr. Ray as teachers. I will be sitting at the feet of Christ, Paul, Abraham, Isaiah and others, and I only know that I will thrill at the new things I learn daily, as I dig into the infinite Source of Wisdom. For me, Heaven will not be a place of idle resting, but it will be a place of inspiring learning and serving."

Mostly for himself, but perhaps for all people who reach a similar milestone of age in their lives, Orvil wrote the following "Prayer On My Eighty-Second Birthday."

Thank you Lord, for this beautiful day,
Help me to live, in thy holy-wise way.
Help me dear Lord, to never forget
That, as is the beauty of sunrise, is the sunset.

Lord, help me to live, not "buried in self,"
But, may I live in a beautiful "altruistic self,"
If I, for God, and humanity, truly do live,
Through my influence in others, I eternally will live.

May all, at my funeral, who would see me,
May they not look in casket, for there I'll not be.
In my casket will be only my "body's house of clay,"
And empty it will be, since I, in death, went away.

And while sad songs at my funeral loved ones sing
I will be rejoicing at the throne of Christ, my King,
And in Heaven's perfect joy I with Christ will be,
Throughout the endless ages of eternity.

At my funeral may songs of joy and peace to heaven raise,
And the name of my Lord, in joy and jubilee, Christ

278

praise!

We all hoped it would be many, many years before that day came. For now, there they sat in their living room, looking out at the beautiful trees blowing in the breeze outside their front door --- Orvil and Alma, side by side, hand in hand, heart with heart. And it's as true now as it was for all those many other years -- home was wherever Orvil chose to hang one of his many hats.

But as would Orvil quickly says, "Sombreros, Don, the word is sombreros."

CHAPTER 21

THE LAST SOMBRERO OF ORVIL REID

Several times in the last few years, Don and Kay were able to visit with Orvil and his dear wife Alma, where they still lived in Ft. Worth. On one of those visits, Don had the holy-ground privilege of spending several days with them, and reading most of the working manuscript of this book aloud to them as they sat in their living room again. What a special joy to see their smiles. What a personal delight to hear their laughter. It wasn't even bad to observe their tears, as they too were able to relive once more, some of the most important years of their lives through this book. More than once during those

280

glory-filled days, Orvil said to Don through his wide and endearing smile, "Why Don, you know more about me than I can even remember about myself." Don took those words and his reactions to imply that Orvil was inwardly pleased with what he was doing to present him, and the many ways the Lord had used him in his life to reach out to others. Don assured him at that time that he would still do everything within his power to tell those reading his story how the Lord did take that "nobody like him from the nowhere from which he came and did so many wonderful things through him for His Kingdom's work." The last time Don saw him, Orvil gripped his hand so tightly in that vice-like grip that it almost hurt, holding it there for some time before he could speak. Holding his face close to Don's, tears were welling up in both their eyes. With that voice so soft and gentle, Orvil quietly whispered the simple but profound words, which Don knew expressed much, much more than the two simple syllables they sounded, when he said with that voice over-running with emotion, "Thank you."

The Reids lived in that home in Ft. Worth about as long as they'd lived in any other single place. The small oak tree in the front yard grew so large that it cast a giant shadow over the front of the house when its branches were loaded with bushy green leaves. When Orvil was at home, his favorite spot was a large recliner, strategically placed so he'd have a good view of the sun filtering through the leaves of that tree. In later months when he was bed-ridden, he was propped up in a hospital bed in the living room, and enjoyed watching the neighbors coming and going and the leaves on his favorite tree doing the same.

One month after Don read them the manuscript of the book on that late spring afternoon, he and Kay were in Ft. Worth again. Orvil was experiencing more physical problems. One year later, Don was able to place in Orvil and Alma's hands, a full copy of the "all-but-finished" manuscript of the book you have just read. Shortly thereafter, Alma returned that manuscript, along with her usual helpful suggestions. Before the final draft could be returned to them, Orvil died on September 9, 1994.

Don and Kay joined many others in his church for Orvil's victorious memorial service. He couldn't keep from thinking how many times in his earthly life, Orvil had "set out on a run." Now, he had run his final race, a good race, he had now finished the course. Always before he'd had to keep his eyes on the goal line, and press toward the mark and the prize. Now he was over that final finish line and the prize was now his. No one could take this eternal victory away from him. There was no doubt that he was now an important part of that significant cloud of witnesses on the sidelines cheering the rest of us on. Orvil had reached his long awaited heavenly home and along with hearing the words about his being a good and faithful servant, he was now wearing the last of his many sombreros, this one in the form of that crown of life reserved for them that love the Lord.

"From Alma's Newsletter Christmas 1995: How do you go on after losing a spouse (married over fifty years)? After our daughter's death, Orvil and I began working in Mexico as a team and continued that way. I was wonderful being together in camps, world mission conferences, and overseas ministry. Exercise? We did it together. In a message from Dr. and Mrs. Russell Dilday, after Orvil's homegoing, Mrs. Dilday said that she missed seeing us every morning, on James Avenue, holding hands, going for our walk or jog.

"In the months I looked after Orvil when he became bedfast, he wanted me by his side and he wanted his weights under his bed. On that 550-mile jog in 1976, he counted steps for a mile. When he had to go to the hospital, my cot was in his room and I could hear him counting, day and night, even though he was unconscious and could not talk, he counted from one to nearly one hundred, over and over. He was again on a jog, this time counting his steps to his heavenly home, where he arrived September 9 of last year at the age of 86."

There's only one final footnote to be written. Alma lived a wonderful and full life following Orvil's death. She was lonely, but her church friends and missionary friends kept her going for many years. She lived in that same little house for her remaining years on earth. Kay and Don visited her there as often as they could. Each time was an extremely special time for all of them. They all regretted this book wasn't published before Orvil's death, but had the joy of knowing he had read it and enjoyed it. They hoped it might make it into publication before Alma went on to be with the Lord. That didn't happen either, for not too long ago, Alma Ervin Reid joined Orvil in that great cloud of heavenly witnesses, where she too received the Lord's personal praise and well-done words for her many years of faithful service, as well as her part in the life, work, and ministry involved with the many sombreros of Orvil Reid.